T0301718

I found the book to be both wide-ranging and accessible. It is a reflection of the authors' strong grounding in the key academic research in this area yet anchored in practice and highly readable. This is in part a reflection of the fact that the ideas have been refined through iteration with many cohorts of participants in Executive and Masters programs at the Nanyang Business School, who are themselves experienced practitioners in diverse roles and organizations. For opportunity identification, a wide range of approaches are introduced, each illustrated with several interesting and current examples.

The book goes further, beyond opportunity identification to development of the ideas identified, using a design thinking approach, which offers a helpful framework and set of guiding principles, fleshed out with the help of succinct examples. The book also reflects the reality of the challenging times we live in and offers principles for dealing with the turbulence and unpredictability, drawing on the authors' extensive fieldwork with entrepreneurs and innovators.

I enjoyed the closing chapters on trends — digital, sustainability, demographic and more — again both for its broad sweep, anchored in today's realities, and constructive opportunity orientation. I found several ideas popping into my head relating to units that I oversee as I read the book — a sign that the book is achieving its objective of helping anyone who is interested in finding opportunities to solve problems through innovation.

Prof Soh Wai Lin, Christina
Dean, College of Business
Nanyang Business School
Nanyang Technological University, Singapore

The authors through their many years of research have pieced together a structured process that can help entrepreneurs navigate their start-up journey, from the stage of ideation to developing the right business models and strategies. With the rapidly changing world, it is important for business owners and entrepreneurs to understand the trends that affect their industries and how in turn, these affect all the stakeholders, and then to come out with a game-plan for their business to succeed. The book helps frame these in perspective that can be very useful to get clarity among the clutter caused by the many disruptions we are seeing. Applying design thinking, as the authors advocate, will help business owners in problem solving.

Whether in good or bad times, there are always many opportunities out there and it is important that we can spot these opportunities. This book is a good guide for entrepreneurs and business owners on spotting opportunities and turning those into innovative business models and businesses. The many case studies and examples the authors have added in the book give very useful insights on real life applications of the approach suggested in the book. A great book on Innovation!

Mr Inderjit Singh Dhaliwal
Former Member of Parliament, Singapore

Identifying opportunities is one of the most challenging aspects of digital innovation and enterprise. It requires skills, intuition, and people-centred thinking. Try asking ChatGPT to come up with innovative business ideas! In this book, Professor Boh Wai Fong and Dr Thara Ravindran have presented an elegant, 3-pronged approach that would guide business or social innovation. First, looking inward on the problem that a prospective innovator is trying to solve. Second, looking outward at what customers and users really need; followed by where competitors are trending towards. And third, looking beyond typical planning horizons with technology and market scenarios that allow enterprises to seize unanticipated opportunities.

It is rare for a book of this title to be research-based, practice-oriented and full of actionable theories. It is rarer for authors to take their keen insights from observations of over 500 clients from around the global economic spectrum. The result is a very readable and credible reference that serves as a comprehensive guide for business as well as social innovators in the build-back-better paradigm in the mass digital transformation that is taking place post-Covid.

Prof Ravi S. Sharma
Professor of Technological Innovation,
Zayed University, UAE

If you are looking for easily digestible yet practical suggestions on how to succeed in your start-up journey, or want to appreciate what this journey is like, this is the book for you! Professor Boh and Dr Ravindran distil the latest cutting-edge research on entrepreneurship providing the reader with recommendations that are based on rigorous evidence. Particularly enjoyable were the stories of many companies used to illustrate and bring to life the learning points.

The book starts with recommendations on how one can ideate, from looking within, looking inward, outward, and beyond, providing a comprehensive guide on the million-dollar question — how does one come up with business ideas? They then take us through the use of design thinking process to further develop these ideas.

There are numerous other suggestions on succeeding in the start-up space that are seldom mentioned in other such books. For example, the use of options — making small bets — as a strategy to go into different business areas without over-stretching resources; use of bricolage — purposing resources — as a way to overcome resource constraints; and a detailed description of various partnering models.

Especially insightful were the topics on the latest developments that entrepreneurs should be aware of. Professor Boh and Dr Ravindran detailed the use digital technologies that entrepreneurs can use to provide greater customer immersiveness and personalization. Beyond digital technologies, they explained various social, economic, and technological trends — such as social consciousness of consumers, Internet of Things, and post-pandemic practices — that every entrepreneur must consider. And in numerous instances they provided illustrations of how the business model could look like to tackle these challenges.

A highly recommended read for every entrepreneur and for those who want to understand what entrepreneurship and innovation processes look like.

Prof Foo Maw Der
Professor, Nanyang Business School
Director, NTU Entrepreneurship Academy (NTUpreneur)
Director, Asian Business Case Centre

Quite an engaging read.

Perhaps it's the Mechanical Engineer in me that still has a soft spot for design and innovation...

I would fully recommend this book to all would-be entrepreneurs as being a practical compendium of ways to turn ideas into reality.

Whereas many books on this subject are prescriptive, the authors of this volume have provided various alternative approaches and buttressed them with actual examples making it more useful and beneficial.

I'm confident this book will become required reading for entrepreneurship courses at our institutions.

Mr Dileep Nair
Diplomat
Former UN Under-Secretary-General

This is a timely masterpiece and is a must-read for entrepreneurs aiming to be impactful in establishing PDOs (purpose-driven organisation) to scale innovation amidst the current great shift.

We are living on the edge of a digital genesis awakening.

This book provides great insights and wisdom to help crystalise the "why", "how", and "what" on future proofing business ventures!

Ms Rachel Ooi
Former Chief Growth Officer CXM APAC Dentsu;
International Bestselling Author #unshaken

Identifying Business Opportunities Through Innovation

Identifying Business Opportunities Through Innovation

Wai Fong Boh

Thara Ravindran

Nanyang Technological University, Singapore

World Scientific

EW JERSEY • LONDON • SINGAPORE • BEIJING • SHANGHAI • HONG KONG • TAIPEI • CHENNAI • TOKYO

Published by

World Scientific Publishing Co. Pte. Ltd.

5 Toh Tuck Link, Singapore 596224

USA office: 27 Warren Street, Suite 401-402, Hackensack, NJ 07601

UK office: 57 Shelton Street, Covent Garden, London WC2H 9HE

Library of Congress Cataloging-in-Publication Data
Names: Boh, Wai Fong, author. | Ravindran, Thara, author.
Title: Identifying business opportunities through innovation / Wai Fong Boh,
    Thara Ravindran, Nanyang Technological University, Singapore.
Description: Hackensack, NJ : World Scientific Publishing Company Co Pte Ltd, [2023] |
    Includes bibliographical references and index.
Identifiers: LCCN 2023007867 (print) | LCCN 2023007868 (ebook) |
    ISBN 9789811260278 (hardcover) | ISBN 9789811260285 (ebook) |
    ISBN 9789811260292 (ebook other)
Subjects: LCSH: Entrepreneurship. | Management--Technological innovations. |
    Strategic planning. | Success in business.
Classification: LCC HB615 .B654 2023 (print) | LCC HB615 (ebook) |
    DDC 338/.04--dc23/eng/20230310
LC record available at https://lccn.loc.gov/2023007867
LC ebook record available at https://lccn.loc.gov/2023007868

British Library Cataloguing-in-Publication Data
A catalogue record for this book is available from the British Library.

We acknowledge the support of Nanyang Technological University Tier 1 MOE Research Grant RG66 –19 for the research work cited in this book

For any available supplementary material, please visit
https://www.worldscientific.com/worldscibooks/10.1142/12963#t=suppl

Desk Editor: Kura Sunaina

Typeset by Stallion Press
Email: enquiries@stallionpress.com

Printed in Singapore

Preface

If you are an aspiring entrepreneur or a newly initiated one trying to figure out the path to traverse in the course of an uncertain journey, then this book is for you. If you are a manager looking to manage a business effectively, you will likely find some useful tips in this book. If you are a student of entrepreneurship or business or simply someone who has an interest in finding out more about how to start an enterprise or how to identify and develop new business opportunities, you will likely benefit from this book.

The book aims to serve as a guide on ideation and execution of a business idea and offers help in navigating the hurdles that would emerge in its course. We present lessons and insights gleaned from a multi-year research project which explored how entrepreneurs and managers went about identifying business opportunities and managing their enterprises. In the course of this research, we collected quantitative data and interviewed more than 500 subjects on various aspects of developing and running an enterprise.

The findings were often interesting and at times intriguing and counter intuitive. We were able to distill many principles through our research and we are excited to share these through this book. The ideas and findings covered here have not only been published in reports and papers, but also discussed and shared extensively with practicing entrepreneurs in classrooms over the last decade. This we believe has provided stronger validity to our findings and it is our hope that you benefit from the same.

Select examples from our research and cases from around the world are used to illustrate some of the key principles that guide ideation as well as execution of a business idea. Drawing on these examples, we also delve into how companies have managed to transform themselves and remained afloat, especially during these difficult times.

The book offers effective tips on identifying potential business opportunities, developing business ideas with a well-defined and systematic approach, and exploiting emerging trends and patterns.

As the world goes through a period of uncertainty and turbulence caused by various external shocks, it would be no surprise if an aspiring entrepreneur feels discouraged enough to give up. This book reminds you that turbulence and challenges also bring along opportunities that can be exploited.

The following would summarize the key features of this book:

Research based — The content of the book primarily comes from several longitudinal mixed methods research studies, funded by research grants, examining more than 500 entrepreneurs and managers. Evidence based insights is therefore a key feature of the book.

Grounded in practical frameworks — The book presents several theories and frameworks, derived from rigorous empirical studies and broader academic literature, that will provide a systematic guide for entrepreneurs and managers.

Practice oriented — The approach and presentation of the book is practice oriented and is therefore readily applicable in real-world situations.

In these pandemic ridden times, this book would no doubt be a useful resource for entrepreneurs and managers looking to ride out the key challenges and emerge as survivors and successful business leaders.

Writing the book has been an extremely satisfying journey for us. We hope that you will enjoy reading the book as much as we have enjoyed putting it together.

About the Authors

Wai Fong Boh is President's Chair and Professor of Information Systems at Nanyang Technological University (NTU) in Singapore. She is currently the Deputy Dean of Nanyang Business School (NBS), Director of Information Management Research Centre at NBS, and serves as co-Director for both Singapore Agri-Food Innovation Lab (SAIL @ NTU) and NTU Centre in Computational Technologies for Finance (CCTF). She received her PhD from the Tepper School of Business at the Carnegie Mellon University. Prof Boh conducts research in the areas of knowledge and innovation management, entrepreneurship, and blockchain. She has published many articles in top management journals including Management Science, MIS Quarterly, Academy of Management Journal, and Research Policy. She has also won multiple awards, including best papers in journals, conferences, and best IS professor in Asia. Professor Boh is a seasoned and versatile instructor who teaches at both undergraduate and graduate levels. She has spoken in multiple industry conferences, and specializes in research and conducting training for entrepreneurs, managers, and employees in areas related to innovation and entrepreneurship. Professor Boh is also a much sought after trainer in entrepreneurship and innovation both in the private and government sectors and is often interviewed and quoted in the media. Prof Boh is currently the Senior Editor of MIS Quarterly, and has been an Associate Editor for Management Science and ISR. She is on the editorial board of multiple top journals, including Journal of Management Information Systems, and Journal of Strategic Information Systems.

Thara Ravindran is currently a Research Fellow at the Information and Management Research Center (IMARC), Nanyang Business School, Nanyang Technological University. Dr Ravindran has a PhD in Information Systems from the Wee Kim Wee School of Communication and Information, NTU, and a Masters in Knowledge Management (Lexis-Nexis Gold medal winner) from the same school. Over the years, Dr Ravindran has worked on several projects in the areas of entrepreneurship, innovation, and strategy, including an NRF funded project that examined the effect of innovation practices of SMEs and start-ups in Singapore on firm performance, a global robotics strategy for Continental Automotive using SWOT analysis of key sectors and a strategic plan based on projected market turnovers in food delivery within ASEAN besides projects examining the usability and adoption of delivery robots. Moreover, Dr Ravindran is experienced in grant writing being part of a team that won SGD 2 million grant for a smart city project sponsored by MND. She has co-authored a recent paper published on entrepreneurship against the context of COVID-19 as well as several others in the domain of social network use which are often cited.

Contents

Chapter 1

A Model of Business Opportunity Identification

"We must open the doors of opportunity. But we must also equip our people to walk through those doors." — Lyndon B. Johnson

An entrepreneurial opportunity is made of a set of ideas, beliefs, and actions that enable the introduction of goods, services, and raw materials as well as the organizing of methods to access markets where none existed (Sarasvathy *et al.*, 2003). Identification of a business opportunity is thus the starting point of any entrepreneurial journey. This step attempts to answer the most basic and pressing question on most aspiring entrepreneurs' minds: "What can I make, provide, or sell that people would want to buy?" Answering this question is the key to laying the foundation to an enterprise. Often this stage has the power to make or break a business and hence the need to deliberate on this.

So, where do you start? By looking around, of course. An opportunity might present itself in the form of a persistent problem, irritant, or inconvenience. It may be faced by oneself or by those in the immediate environment such as family members or co-workers. Have you ever wondered why something could not be done by an everyday gadget, equipment, appliance, or a software? Or made easier? Or less troublesome? Or why an obvious design oversight of a daily-use artefact has been driving users to suffer in silence?

There is almost always a hidden opportunity in these day-to-day problems you stumble upon. But of course, only if you are sufficiently tuned in and adequately inclined to mull over possible solutions.

Women's safety has been a global problem for centuries. The birth of InvisaWear, a US-based specialized jewelry was triggered by an event that happened in the life of founders Ray and Rajia. One night, the couple was returning from an event when a car full of men pulled up, rolled down the window, and started making inappropriate comments. At one point, the men stopped the car and one of them started to get out. Fortunately, Rajia was able to get away, unharmed. This traumatic event channeled Rajia's thoughts towards building a product that would ensure safety for women trapped in similar situations. Rajia had earlier explored available safety devices that provide S.O.S solutions, but they were either too big and bulky or displayed a "panic button" too prominently. Ray and Rajia wanted a stylish, discreet S.O.S device, ideal for everyday wear. Thus, InvisaWear was born![1]

We call this form of opportunity identification "Looking Inward". It happens when opportunities present themselves within an entrepreneur's immediate personal environment. Opportunities can also emerge as you engage with other entities, systems, or processes as part of their day-to-day work, within the confines of their home or work.

1. Looking Inward

In order to best exploit this kind of opportunity, you need to pay attention to events that happen within your personal environment: Personal experiences with systems or gadgets, customer complaints,

---

[1] https://www.invisawear.com/pages/our-mission

and recurring problems that may be widely encountered by others around, to name a few. Often these present interesting challenges, which may lead to opportunities for viable business ventures.

Using Personal Experiences and Observing People

In our National Research Fund sponsored study of Asian entrepreneurs undertaken in 2015, we identified several business opportunities that were triggered by personal experiences. For example, one aspiring entrepreneur felt challenged by having to manage multiple cards, user IDs, and complex passwords all within a day's work. This persistent problem gave rise to his business idea. He developed a mobile app for companies that would help manage staff access to systems during hiring and resignations. The app allowed access to newly hired employees through adding their phone number and reversed this when he or she resigned through deleting the same.

Another sniffed out an opportunity when he observed an interesting pattern of behavior within his circle of friends. He saw that there was an increasing number of people making requests for items available in different countries with friends who were traveling abroad. This observation prompted him to develop an ecommerce aggregator that gathered personal purchase requests and matched them with travelers.

A third one observed his colleagues using a spreadsheet to take note of seasonal credit card promotions. This observation triggered an idea which he used to develop a system that aggregated credit card promotions.

Solving Routine Problems

Entrepreneurs working within a given environment may come across problems that affect them directly or others they work with. When an entrepreneurial mind tackles such problems, new business opportunities open up.

Mismatch between system functionality and user requirement

Existing systems may fail to support an employee's work routine effectively. Likewise, an unaddressed user requirement may trigger search for a solution that could transform into a business idea.

Here is an example: While working on a project involving a CRM system, Jim, a young entrepreneur we spoke to discovered that it was unable to interface with his email. This in turn, prompted him and his colleagues to go into a problem-solving mode, resulting in the development of an extension that addressed this shortcoming. The extension started to become popular internally amongst colleagues who faced similar issues. As Jim realized that satisfied users were willing to pay for the patch, he recognized that there was a business opportunity and went on to develop it into a commercial product.

Ineffective existing solution

Sometimes, existing solutions to operational problems do not offer satisfactory resolution. This may also present a potential business opportunity.

Amal, an entrepreneur in the oil and gas industry had observed the limitations of the traditional corrosion prevention mechanisms used in his line of work to protect equipment. Amal wanted a better anti-corrosion solution that would ensure longer life for the equipment. He knew that by providing better rust protection over a longer period of time, there would be bigger cost savings for the equipment owners. In his search for a good solution, Amal tried out several and found that none of them worked well. He eventually discovered one offered by an overseas vendor, which worked better than all the other solutions he had tried. To his surprise, his industry peers in Southeast Asia were not aware of this solution. This persuaded Amal to reach out to the vendor to negotiate an exclusive distribution agreement for the ASEAN region. Needless to say, this became a key component of Amal's newly launched anti-corrosion services business.

2. Looking Outward

Entrepreneurs find opportunities within their external environment as they interact with entities in the value chain: customers, suppliers, partners, or affiliates within the industry at large. Such opportunities to interface with stakeholders outside of routine work and within the value chain could trigger entrepreneurial activity in various ways.

Interacting with Customers

Observing customers and interacting with them can help entrepreneurs identify business opportunities. Customer feedback, in particular, is a valuable source of information that enables improvements which can lead to opportunities.

Tim, one of our study participants, ran a business selling sensors designed to improve the performance of tennis players. Maintaining regular contact with tennis coaches had helped Tim gather feedback which benefitted his venture in many ways. The firm had initially positioned themselves as a sports accessory provider. However, through these interactions, Tim was able to identify the need for a mobile application to provide a service to complement their initial product. This was a relatively new one in the domain.

Lending a Sympathetic Ear to End-Users

Opportunities often emerge when entrepreneurs empathetically engage with their end-users. This allows them to zoom in on the user's pain points and go on to generate creative solutions.

The founder of a firm in the healthcare sector reports a similar experience. In the course of his interactions with hospitals, clinics, and patients, founder Gregory identified a common and pressing problem faced by hemodialysis patients. The patients, Gregory realized, were in need of a quick, inexpensive, and non-invasive way of monitoring "stenosis", a condition that results in the narrowing of the blood vessel used for dialysis, at home. This urged him and his co-founders to address the unmet patient need: The team developed a blood pressure cuff that monitored the condition. Eventually, a business venture was set up to commercialize the solution.

We shall discuss how firms can identify opportunities through interactions with users, customers, and suppliers in greater detail in Chapter 3 which deals with design thinking.

Observing or Learning From the Competitors

Competitors can also be a good source of ideas for new business opportunities. It is sometimes worthwhile to emulate their good practices. Mark, an entrepreneur who set up an online content service was keenly watching competitors operating in the domain to understand how they monetized their web traffic. His aim was to identify similar opportunities for his own venture. Likewise, a law firm observed that its competitors often monitored international rankings of law firms and invested resources into ensuring that they performed well in the criteria used by the ranking agencies. By doing this, the firm consciously attempted to match the standards set by the high ranked law firms so that it could improve their legitimacy and reputation.

Yet, sometimes it may be advisable for firms to avoid what their competitors do and remain guided by their own philosophies and ethos. This is because competitors' activities could often be reminders of mistakes to avoid. A school providing enrichment classes for students observed that a key competitor often marketed flexi services to meet the convenience of the parents. They claimed that there was no limit to the number of make-up classes if their children missed a session. In actuality, the number of classes available for make-up were limited in availability. Once they realized this, the school made a conscious effort to avoid such misrepresentation, as they believed in honoring the promises made to clients.

Sometimes, paying attention to competition will point entrepreneurs to gaps which in turn present opportunities. For instance, Stanley, an entrepreneur in the logistics industry observed that competitors in the region typically offered local delivery services within three–five working days, a norm in the industry dating back to 20 years. This presented an opportunity for the entrepreneur to offer an express delivery service, which differentiated him from the competition.

Tuning to Industry News and Organized Networking Events

Keeping up to date with industry news as well as participating in networking events may help entrepreneurs spot and develop business opportunities. This allows them to be informed about the latest trends and stay connected with key players in the industry.

Industry news presents business opportunities in many ways, especially when it comes to meeting market demands. For example, when they read about the surging demand for COVID-19 test kits in Singapore, suppliers like All Eights (Singapore) Pte. Ltd. distributed DIY test kits for those who could not take Polymerase Chain Reaction (PCR) and Antigen Rapid Tests (ART).[2] And when news about ART kit testing being made mandatory for employees in Singapore came out, ART kit distributor SPD Scientific Pte. Ltd. took the opportunity to widen its target market by reaching out to higher-density industries.[3]

Networking events are a great way for businesses to gain contacts and make connections with various stakeholders in their industry. Most such events are organized for a specific purpose or with an industry focus. For example, the hybrid event "Fostering Innovation Towards a More Sustainable Forest Sector in Europe" organized by Rosewood Networking brings together players in the European forestry sector to explore possibilities for long-term sustainability. Besides offering networking opportunities and updates on activities within the sector, such events also serve as a learning platform for entrepreneurs.[4] Sometimes, reports and networking sessions simply

---

[2] https://www.businesstimes.com.sg/garage/suppliers-expect-diy-covid-test-kits-to-take-off-amid-heightened-demand-for-mass-testing

[3] https://t-hub.co/about-us/

[4] https://efi.int/events/rosewood40-final-event-fostering-innovation-towards-more-sustainable-forest-sector-europe

serve as sources of information that plant the seeds of an enterprise in an aspiring mind.

Ajmal, one of our participants, had one such story to share. It was through a networking session that this entrepreneur learned about the difficulties faced by smaller firms in providing employee welfare benefits such as insurance, healthcare, and discounts. At the same time, Ajmal had read news reports on how the special offers and discounts announced by retailers across Singapore had low take-up rates. Accordingly, Ajmal launched a portal that consolidated special offers from various retailers which could be used by smaller firms interested in providing staff benefits in the form of coupons and discounts at no additional cost.

3. Looking Beyond

Entrepreneurs and managers can spot opportunities by looking beyond their immediate environments. However, this requires them to expose themselves to new knowledge within unfamiliar domains and geographic regions. They need to pay attention to other industries and understand the latest trends. They also need to follow emerging patterns, innovations as well as technological advancements in these domains. The entrepreneurs we spoke to reported how they developed novel business ideas into viable ventures through the following means.

Looking at Other Industries or Countries

Observing how other sectors or countries do business, entrepreneurs could be inspired to develop new business ideas. Thus, visits and learning trips abroad help to plant the seeds of entrepreneurship in business aspirants.

For instance, observing how other sectors were shifting to healthier choices enabled one businessman to differentiate his bakery business with healthy snack options. The company had traditionally offered snacks — including curry puffs and other pastries that are deep-fried. By observing the trend towards healthier options, the company decided to open a chain of cafes that offer lower calorie baked savories, rather than the conventional deep-fried ones. They also positioned themselves strategically in hospitals where such products may be in demand.

In another example, a Singapore entrepreneur was inspired by the wide use of digital signages in Taiwan, where his frequent trips took him. During the time, such signages were a rarity in Singapore. He, therefore, saw an opportunity to make and sell digital signages locally where the concept was entirely new. Subsequently, he went ahead to set up his business in the sector.

A serial entrepreneur we met admitted to getting his business idea after a spontaneous sharing at an overseas conference in China. He was there to share his knowledge relating to sustainability and was surprised at the overwhelming interest in the topic. Although he was not thinking of setting up a business at that point, the interest from the audience led him to start a business relating to recycling later.

Integrating Across Industry Sectors

Transferring ideas across industry sectors can sometimes lead to business opportunity identification. This requires entrepreneurs to be alert to pain points in one industry that can be solved by solutions from another.

Sometimes opportunities arise from actively considering how a promising solution from one sector or industry may be applied to another. Allan, who worked in the fresh foods industry, had come up with a packaging solution that maintained the freshness of food in the course of running his operations. Believing there could be other application areas, he searched for opportunities in other domains where freshness and moisture of products is a priority. Allan zoomed in on the beauty industry as one where his solution might be useful.

This process of connecting the dots across domains requires the entrepreneur to be able to take a broader view of things. For example, a bio certified natural ingredient from the farming sector has several unique features that can be exploited in other sectors. Bio certification deals with healthy food growing, organic methods of crop cultivation (Kononets and Treiblmaier, 2021).

Ecocert is an organic certification standard which ensures that 95% of the ingredients are natural.[5] No synthetic fragrances, colors, petroleum derivatives, polymers, parabens, or other potentially harmful substances can be used in these certified products. In agriculture and handicraft processing, the certification ensures high quality of raw materials used. Hence, a certified agriproduct, such as bee wax, resin, or an extract, can be safely ported over to, say, the personal hygiene sector. Beauty and skincare products or toothpastes could use such certified ingredients.

Another example can be seen in India-based Jayalaxmi Agro-Tech (JAT). Having grown up in a farm, founder Anand Babu Chitav had an idea of how stressful farming has been traditionally. When he returned home after spending time abroad for 15 years, he found that nothing had changed in the farming sector back home. It was still fraught with issues such as high input costs and little information or even misinformation. He also saw how, even when IT was used widely in all other sectors, it was underutilized in farming. Mobile technologies were exploding in rural India. However, they had not been exploited to modernize farming yet. In an archetypal illustration of looking beyond, Chitav saw how this presented an opportunity to use technology to address farmers' issues. He then went on to set up JAT, a company which offered mobile farming app-based solutions to address common problems faced by farmers.[6]

Following Technological Trends

Technological trends can present business opportunities for entrepreneurs who are keen observers of technological advancements. For instance, we interviewed an entrepreneur who ventured into

---

[5] https://www.be-ecocentric.com/html/labels-bio
[6] https://hbsp.harvard.edu/product/IMB731-PDF-ENG

digital health because he saw that new technologies offered novel ways of handling needs within the sector. He realized that such technologies were not being exploited adequately in the Singapore context. This gave birth to his healthcare web business, which offered online outpatient care and related services by creating a nexus of healthcare providers, insurance companies and policyholders. This helped repair the siloed healthcare system by allowing the value chain to work seamlessly together.

Scanning for Emerging Market Trends

Emerging global and regional trends also present entrepreneurs with new business opportunities. Different markets present diverse opportunities, so actively scanning them can help entrepreneurs develop viable business ideas. For example, the trend of consumerism and lifestyle changes in emerging markets such as Myanmar and Vietnam gave an entrepreneur the idea of setting up franchises of F&B outlets in these markets.

In another instance, Anhui LIGOO New Energy Technology Co., Ltd (LIGOO), a Chinese firm set up in 2010, started off by offering an efficient Battery Management System (BMS) targeted at the communications and coal mining sectors. Towards 2012, as they began to make a mark in this field, they noticed a strong governmental push towards the adoption of New Energy Vehicles (NEVs). As part of this push, the government launched several initiatives, including the "863 Program" the National Hi-Tech Research & Development Program of China. The aim was to boost innovation in high-tech sectors so that Chinese firms can enjoy a lead position in the world market. The country had also successfully established a framework for the development of EVs. Spurred by the successful use of EVs during the Beijing Olympics as well as a series of government sponsored incentive schemes, China had developed into a leading manufacturer of EVs. LIGOO capitalized on this trend to successfully expand from their BMS business into the NEV sector.

Swimming Against the Tide

While it is important to identify major trends, it may not always be necessary to follow them. In a strategy diametrically opposite to the earlier one, entrepreneurs may also identify opportunities by going against an established trend. In one interesting case, an entrepreneur identified that popular e-learning platforms (such as MOOC) and content providers (such as Udemy) based their business models on the assumption that the Internet will continue to grow and reach a wider audience.

The entrepreneur, however, decided to take a U-turn and went against the trend by designing offline content. The thought came from the realization that there are several regions in the world where Internet access is intermittent, and Internet-based offerings struggle to achieve economies of scale. This was the case even in developed countries, where people still have limited access to the Internet. In such markets where connectivity was an issue yet e-learning was in demand, he believed an offline approach would work.

Overall, as illustrated in Figure 1, these three approaches — looking inward, looking outward, and looking beyond — represent important ways by which managers and entrepreneurs can identify new business opportunities.

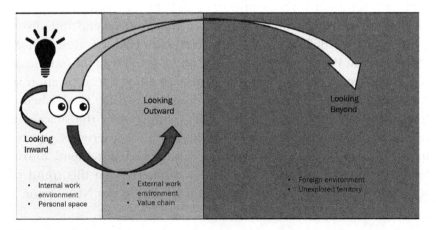

Figure 1: Sources of Business Opportunity Identification

Chapter 2

Key Actors in Opportunity Identification

"A wise person knows that there is something to be learned from everyone."

As a business, you are never a self-sufficient island of activities and knowledge. Your firm interacts with many external and internal entities for purposes beside transacting goods, services, and money. So, who are these key entities you should pay attention to, so that you may get inspired to come up with ideas and opportunities? The first to consider are the key actors in your industry value chain whom you interact with either directly or indirectly.

The usual suspects include customers and suppliers, who are invaluable sources of business knowledge. Then, there are the competitors whose activities define the external business environment. Competitors also have an important role in inspiring business ideas as they operate alongside your firm, offering distinct products and services in their own ways.

As direct beneficiaries of the value-add that your firm provides, your customers and suppliers are reservoirs of specialized knowledge relating to your products and services. It is easy for you to get feedback from these stakeholders through regular interactions with them. Information about competitors, on the other hand, is less readily accessible. Often, such information can only be inferred through what is available in the marketplace, including products, services, promotional activities, and public financial statements. Yet, all these entities help your firm identify new business opportunities, as each one is in a unique position to inspire thoughts that could eventually lead to novel ideas. We elaborate on how this is possible with the help of some examples in the sections that follow.

1. Customers

Customers are the immediate beneficiaries of your products and services. They use, consume, or interact with what your business offers to address their needs. With repeated use, they develop insights about your offerings, which can be a vital source of business knowledge that no amount of lab-based testing or market research can match. As an entrepreneur, you can benefit from interacting with your end users by gathering their feedback on your offerings, listening to their needs and pain points, or even getting inspired by their creative ideas.

This is reflected in the viewpoint of innovation expert, Eric von Hippel, who believes that users are often the first source of new products.[1] Hippel's "free innovation paradigm" illustrates the innovations developed by consumers. Free innovation involves innovations developed by consumers who are self-rewarded for their efforts, and who give their designs away "for free". Why are consumers a good source of innovation? Because they are willing to give away their ideas developed using their unpaid discretionary time. Additionally, they are self-rewarded as they expect nothing other than personal utility, learning, and fun from developing these ideas. The icing on the cake is that there are no hassles of monetary transactions and intellectual property rights attached to using this source of ideas. Hippel calls this a "simple grassroots innovation process" (von Hippel, 2016).

---

[1] https://sloanreview.mit.edu/article/the-user-innovation-revolution/

The focus on users as lead innovators acknowledges the view that problems often push users into developing hacks or workarounds which may inspire solutions that can become great opportunities. According to Design Guru, Donald Norman, workarounds are "the soul of innovation ... where the answers lie." Through observing how people circumvent the problems they face routinely entrepreneurs can be inspired to come up with novel business ideas.

A workaround is an action taken or a process developed by someone with a view to solving a problem or addressing a "pain point". Often it is performed to get around a block or bottleneck in a workflow and thereby achieve a desired goal. Fundamentally, we can view this as an ingenuous temporary solution. Workarounds often involve unconventional use of materials or items to solve an immediate problem. Sometimes users also cobble together everyday products with other items to address a shortcoming in one of their daily use products. While this ensures the task goal is met, there is a danger that the action deviates from the norm, protocol or standards established.

Workarounds can be seen all around us as people tend to devise them every day without consciously trying, in an attempt to quickly fix a problem. These are often created for either of the following two reasons: a day-to-day problem does not have any available solutions, or a solution exists but is simply too expensive to obtain.

Users who create workarounds are articulating an unmet need in the existing solution. For example, Nokia's idea to build a penlight into their phones came from an observation of users in China who used mobile phones as a source of light. The observations revealed a workaround which included a hidden need. When phone users needed to get to a light source in the dark to read or search for something their hack was to use the light from the cellphone screen. This presented an opportunity to create an enhanced product that would cater to this unconventional use of the phone.

Often, clever, high frequency users of day-to-day products devise means of getting the best out of them. For example, market surveys have reported that some consumers are in the habit of keeping shampoo bottles or ketchup bottles upside down just so that it is easier for them to get the last bits out of the containers. Taking a cue from this unconventional use of the bottles, various businesses spotted an opportunity to design bottles with the lids at the bottom.

These examples illustrate that there are hidden opportunities in workarounds as much as problems. Such workarounds can be developed into viable business ideas. These kinds of opportunities are inspired by temporary solutions that creative everyday people conjure up. In such cases, it is highly likely that a permanent or more optimal solution needs to be sought. That is where the business opportunity lies. You just need to look hard enough. Design thinking will provide you with a systematic means of doing that.

> *Hacks and workarounds can inspire creative solutions and, through these, business opportunities.*

In the course of our research on innovation and entrepreneurship in Singapore, we came across much evidence pointing to the importance of observing customers and users to understand their needs and pain points. In some instances, entrepreneurs used this method to expand into adjacent lines of business. An example can be seen in Bus-Inc., a firm that provides entertainment systems for buses. During routine servicing, they noticed that the clients frequently complained about the unruly behaviors of their bus drivers. These complaints sometimes even interfered with the clients' insurance claims, causing delays in processing. Bus-Inc. spotted an opportunity and acted quickly, launching a video surveillance system for buses. Needless to say, the product sold so well that the firm later extended the product to other heavy vehicles.

In another example, Expert Solutions, a consulting business, started off by providing strategic advise to firms. Soon, firm director Peter found out that his clients invariably ended up recruiting a second agency to implement the branding recommendations provided by his firm. Since Peter knew that his team had the requisite expertise to move into brand consulting, he decided to expand their services. Later, Peter also found out that some of them chose to franchise their brands after successfully penetrating the local market. This created another adjacent opportunity for him to expand into, namely, franchising. Peter eventually went on to help broker overseas franchising opportunities for his clients.

Customer feedback oftentimes enables improvements and innovations to solutions that you offer routinely. James, an entrepreneur in the sportswear domain cited his constant interaction with customers as the main source of his ideas for improving his products. James had initially started off by offering tennis sensors to improve player performance. Through regular interactions with tennis coaches he met, James gathered feedback which helped him fine-tune the product's features.

Although the firm had initially positioned itself as a sports accessory provider, customer interactions helped them identify the need for a mobile application to complement their products. The mobile app allowed tennis players to monitor and improve their performance. This was a novelty at the time it was launched.

With external shocks such as the COVID-19 pandemic, it becomes even more important for entrepreneurs to keep up with trends that may be shaping customer buying patterns and behaviors. The pandemic has changed the way people shop. A clear trend of online shopping emerged. While online shopping is not exactly a new trend, its necessity and public perception changed when the pandemic hit the world.

The perception that physical and virtual shopping are two distinct categories that cater to two distinct classes of customers has changed. Grocery shopping was typically a weekly drive to the nearest store while online shopping was only for the busy townsfolk. This trend has undergone a major shift: Currently, online grocery shopping is for everyone. Besides, the view that online shopping is only suitable for certain types of products and services no longer holds. From groceries to health supplies to education, a whole range of products and services are being offered online which brought in a realization that the logic of convenience applies to any product or service that can be offered online. Thus, services such as medical consultation traditionally offered physically have moved online. Businesses can capitalize on knowledge about such trends to spot new opportunities.

> *Do you constantly interact with your customers?*
>
> *Do you receive customer feedback?*
>
> *Do you understand customer needs and pain points?*
>
> *Do your customers share their creative ideas with you?*
>
> *How can you address the above and create business opportunities?*

2. Suppliers

Since the 1990s, suppliers have come to be viewed as valuable collaborators for a business. Effective information sharing between suppliers and businesses can help enable faster development and launch of new products and ensure better quality offerings and cost savings.

Traditionally, the business value chain revolved around the product. In other words, firms looked for suppliers who could provide the components that were required to make the product they designed. However, in recent years, the focus has shifted to what suppliers are able to provide that can enhance a firm's existing line of products. This is especially the case for sectors such as automobiles where customers far outnumber suppliers. We see many innovations in the automobile industry where components such as driverless navigation are prompting revolutionary changes to product designs.

According to a McKinsey report,[2] supplier innovations are effective since they are typically commercialized 40 percent faster than in-house ideas. For example, UK carmaker, Aston Martin, worked

---

[2] https://www.mckinsey.com/business-functions/operations/our-insights/managing-your-external-supply-system-for-innovation

with their US based aerospace supplier, Flexsys, to develop seamless adjustable wings for its high-end models. The key feature of these wings is the flexible material used that provides better aerodynamics and cleaner appearance.

In another example, when they launched a project to reduce their window trim cost, automaker Ford, looked towards their supplier for a suitable solution. The supplier helped by creating a new resin which made the manufacturing process more efficient. The new resin was able to cut out 2,700 gallons of diesel fuel by removing 19,200 truck miles transporting parts between factories. Thus, there were dual benefits from this innovation: Environmental protection and cost reduction.[3]

Although used extensively in the auto manufacturing sector, this form of supplier-based innovations could be applied to other sectors too. Take, for instance, the case of retail giant Walmart. Founder Sam Walton had recognized the importance of big data and had supported an open data sharing policy with their suppliers such as P&G right from the start. This was the reason why the chain was able to grow and outpace their competition. The move also enabled Walmart to improve forecasting as well as management of shelf space and inventory. More recently, collaborating with suppliers allowed Walmart to launch "Get on the Shelf", a competition where aspiring entrepreneurs could win the chance to sell their products on Walmart's website and secure a slot on the prestigious Walmart supplier list. The program allows Walmart to bring new products to their shelves and enables budding entrepreneurs to test out their product ideas and potentially be on Walmart's list of suppliers.[4]

L'Oréal started hosting an event called "Cherry Pack" to innovate with their suppliers in 2010. This was a time when collaborating with suppliers was a rarity in the cosmetics business. The goal of the

---

[3] https://blog.vizibl.co/supplier-innovation-case-studies/
[4] https://www.forbes.com/sites/jacobmorgan/2015/08/03/the-5-types-of-innovation-for-the-future-of-work-pt-3-partner-supplier-innovation/?sh=702cf3821266

event was to facilitate meetings between suppliers and L'Oréal executives to discuss matters like product formulations and ideas for marketing and packaging candidly. The result was that L'Oréal suppliers were able to create unique products for the company which they could then sell. For example, the self-loading pipette used in many L'Oréal products is an example of an innovation born out of their relationship with suppliers.[5]

Specialized suppliers are therefore excellent sources of business knowledge who you can tap into to open up business opportunities. Sharing knowledge and exchanging ideas with your suppliers may trigger ideas for new products, services, or solutions.

In one example, we saw that open sharing of problems with suppliers led to innovations that resolved many issues for a design company, DES-INC. The lack of information on availability of components had resulted in an inefficient design process. This meant that DES-INC would need to repeatedly change their designs based on alternative components proposed by the supplier.

Sensing an opportunity, DES-INC reached out to the supplier to discuss whether a more open approach towards information sharing was possible. This required compromise from both ends, but ultimately led to mutual benefits. DES-INC found that their supplier felt that programs with them required more effort compared to others. This was because DES-INC did not use the standard design blueprint and did not share the list of components that the blueprint demanded. The realization allowed both parties to adopt compromises to facilitate each other's work. First, DES-INC agreed to change their design specifications and blueprint based on the standards used by their supplier and to provide the list of components based on the design. In return, the supplier agreed to share their inventory list with DES-INC so that the latter could create designs which afforded greater visibility on inventory availability.

---

[5] https://www.forbes.com/sites/jacobmorgan/2015/08/03/the-5-types-of-innovation-for-the-future-of-work-pt-3-partner-supplier-innovation/?sh=702cf3821266

This example suggests that while you may have regular interactions with your suppliers, it may not help to take an "us-versus-them" mentality. Instead, viewing each other as partners and trying to understand each other's viewpoints may help you work together to resolve the hurdles. In turn, this may create opportunities to improve processes, solutions, and products for both firms.

> *Do you have formal and informal opportunities to meet and discuss with your suppliers?*
>
> *Do you share and exchange information constantly?*
>
> *Are your suppliers in a position to enhance your existing processes or products?*
>
> *How can you make use of their innovations to improve your business and create new opportunities?*

3. Competitors

Competitors can also be a good source of ideas for business opportunities, even though information about competitors may be less accessible compared to the other entities on your value chain. Knowledge about your competitors can be gained from observing their activities and offerings. On one hand, you may be able to pick up their best practices that could be worthwhile learning from and emulating. On the other, you may find that competitors are salient reminders of what not to do in your industry. In this exercise, it may be worthwhile asking yourself some questions: What are your competitors doing that may be worth emulating? What are your competitors doing that you will want to avoid? What are some gaps that exist based on the offerings provided by your competitors?

Emulating Competitors

Ben, co-founder of an online sales aggregator providing consolidated information on credit card promotions confessed to keenly following his successful competitors. Ben observed how these leaders monetized their online traffic and identified similar opportunities for his own business. The firm had initially struggled to attract traffic and get people to read their content. They overcame this hurdle by studying what their competitors did. However, they made a conscious effort to also differentiate themselves by staying focused on their main value-add of consolidating credit card promotions.

Avoiding Competitors' Mistakes

Sometimes, common mistakes made by your competitors can serve as cautionary tales that may inspire ideas for new businesses. For example, Flipkart, the leading Indian ecommerce company, first sniffed out an opportunity when they noticed that rival Amazon had a relatively poor delivery infrastructure outside of the major metros in India. Founders Sachin Bansal and Binny Bansal, both alumni of the prestigious Indian Institute of Technology and former Amazon employees, saw potential in a model focused on country-wide shipping. Thus, the idea for their successful business was triggered by a desire to address the shortfall in the operations of their major international competitor. The firm targeted aspirational customers in smaller Indian cities and villages where Amazon did not have a strong delivery network at the time. They also offered cash on delivery (CoD) to circumvent the problem of low rates of adoption of credit card and internet-based payments in Indian villages.

Two promising Asian businesses in the hospitality sector — Oyo and Xbed — also have similar stories behind their inception and success. Both businesses were based on the successful Airbnb model but aimed to address the shortcomings of Airbnb.

Xbed, the Chinese firm that was inspired by Airbnb, focused on the security concerns raised by the customers of their rival model. Xbed used automated door locks and offered housekeeping services, both of which catered to common and unaddressed needs of travelers. Additionally, they also connected their customer database to the Chinese police database. This allowed for background checks on customers, much to the relief of the property owners.

As for Oyo, they differentiated themselves from Airbnb by building a chain of self-branded rooms and standardizing services in their budget accommodation. This included clean washrooms, spotless linen, air-conditioned rooms with television, free breakfast, and free Wi-Fi.

Gaps in Competitor Offerings

Closer Home, a Singapore firm in the logistics sector, offered an express delivery service to address a gap in the offerings of their competitors. The entrepreneur, Alan, observed that current delivery service providers typically offered local delivery within three–five working days which has been the status quo for the last two decades. This presented a hidden opportunity for him to offer an express delivery service, differentiating himself from the competition.

> *What are your competitors doing that may be worthwhile imitating or emulating?*
>
> *What are your competitors doing that you would want to avoid?*
>
> *What are some gaps that exist based on the offerings provided by your competitors?*

4. Sharing Within the Network of BoI Actors

In summary, as we slice and dice the opportunity identification framework, we realize that it is important to know who the actors within the frame are and to listen closely to what they have to say. This means maintaining close communication with your customers and striking strategic alliances with your suppliers. Interactions with various stakeholders and how each could inspire business

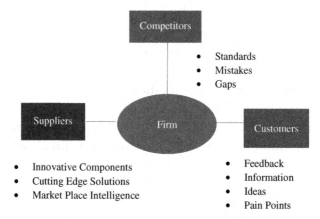

Figure 1:   Stakeholder interactions.

ideas is illustrated in Figure 1. Tapping on informal networks and sources of business intelligence to keep abreast of the practices and offerings of your competitors is also important when it comes to uncovering business opportunities.

Chapter 3

Design Thinking

"If I had an hour to solve a problem, I'd spend 55 minutes thinking about the problem, and 5 minutes thinking about the solutions."
— *Albert Einstein*

So, now you have your business idea. What next? Well, you will now need a means of translating this into a viable business. Successful execution of business ideas requires a deliberate and systematic approach. In Chapter 1, we had established that "problems" are at the center of opportunity identification. Therefore, a problem-solving approach would be appropriate for the translation of ideas into viable business plans. However, do remember that this is not about addressing what people want but rather what they need.

Here we would like to introduce the paradigm of "Design Thinking" as an approach that helps you to identify, define, and better understand the problems and needs of stakeholders. The term "Design Thinking" has been in use as early as 1987, both in theory and practice amongst design practitioners and researchers. Over the years, however, the concept gained widespread interest in domains as diverse as education, management, information technology, business, and medicine.

1. What is Design Thinking?

Design thinking has been defined as an *"analytic and creative process that engages a person in opportunities to experiment, create and prototype models, gather feedback, and redesign"* (Razzouk and Shute, 2012). Terms such as "creative", "experimental", "prototypes", and "feed-back" strike us as characteristics of this approach. In another early definition, design thinking was viewed as a *"human problem-solving behavior further modelled as a search from an initial state, via intermediate states, to the goal state(s)"* (Simon, 1969). Problem-solving with the intention of deriving a solution is the essence of design thinking according to this definition.

Today, design thinking is considered a natural and common human activity that occurs all around much like planning for day-to-day activities (Razzouk and Shute, 2012). The process essentially combines empathy, creativity, and rationality to meet user needs and ensure business success. As such, user need is the starting point of design thinking. The process then goes through an iterative refine-ment phase to ensure the problem is solved systematically and incrementally.

One well-known example of design thinking comes from tooth-brush maker Oral-B.[1] Designers Kim Colin and Sam Hecht were assigned to help Oral-B upgrade their electric toothbrush. The firm had originally wanted the designers to add more functions, such as tracking brushing frequency, observing gum sensitivity, and playing music. Yet, Colin and Hecht decided to understand user problem before finalizing the requirements.

After their interactions with the users, they emerged with a new understanding of the user problem. They found out that brushing teeth was a "neurotic act" as it was an automatic behavior, and an unconscious effort would be made by the person brushing to man-age a deeper anxiety in the course of completing the routine. What this meant was, adding more functionalities to the brush would only serve to stress users. Based on this knowledge, the designers advised the firm to avoid gimmicks and focus on improving the user experi-ence. They recommended two functional enhancements instead.

---

[1] https://online.hbs.edu/blog/post/design-thinking-examples

The first was to make the brushes easier to charge — a feature that traveling users would appreciate. The second was to make it easier for them to order replacement heads. This enhancement supported repeated ordering by connecting the brushes to the users' phones and sending reminder notifications. Needless to say, these two design features were well received by Oral-B users. The example illustrates how a focus on what the user needs rather than what the business wants to do for them can ensure successful design of a product.

Netflix is another firm that has successfully used design thinking many times to grow into a leader in the digital entertainment industry. In their incremental yet rapid growth into the current position, the firm used design thinking to provide services based on unmet customer needs innovatively rather than improving marginally on what is currently available.

Netflix first started as a DVD rental company famously disrupting the Blockbuster model which rented movies through their conventional "brick-and-mortar" stores. They observed that a key customer pain point of Blockbuster and companies with similar models was that they had to drive to the VCD store to pick up and drop off VCDs. Netflix decided to start a DVD selling and rental business by mail (snail mail — involving envelopes and stamps — for those of us who may not know what this means). The company also got rid of late fees which was another pain point for users, as it required users to track the due dates of their DVD rentals. Instead, Netflix offered unlimited discs per month, with no late fees, as long as users held on to either one or two DVDs at any one time. Subsequently, as DVDs became obsolete, Netflix quickly moved on to a then revolutionary idea of demand streaming service which elevated entertainment to an entirely different level.

The story of the development of Tegaderm[2] dressing by 3M illustrates how problems can present opportunities, especially if you focus on needs rather than wants.

---

[2] https://www.3m.com/3M/en_US/particles/all-articles/article-detail/~/tegaderm-dressings-surgery-solution-nurses-need/?storyid=eb703b4a-5f60-4d22-a2f8-912dc43fb8c8

At the start of his career with 3M, back in the 1970s, inventor Steven Heinecke was visiting a local hospital to observe doctors, nurses, and patients, and understand how 3M products can meet the needs of the healthcare sector. There, he followed critical care nurses on their daily rounds and watched them as they attended to their patients. Steven's goal was to understand nurses' pain points and figure out means to address them and make their jobs easier.

Steven noticed that as nurses attended to patients with IV insertions, they ingeniously and tediously applied the gauze and tape in a way that allowed them to keep an eye on the insertion site. They did this so that they could monitor the insertion for signs of potential infection easily. The normal tape which stuck to the area where it was applied to, did not cater to this need.

On talking to the nurses, Steven found out that they would have liked a gentler adhesive that allowed them to remove the bandage and reapply it multiple times without any hassles. If he had defined his statement based on what the nurses said, he would probably have defined the problem statement as generating better tape for the nurses. Instead, he took a step back and realized that the fundamental need of the nurses is to have an easy way to monitor the insertion site for any infection. Based on this problem statement, he came up with a unique solution that would address it. Steven realized that a transparent dressing would enable the nurses to monitor the IV insertions easily without going through the hassle of removing and reapplying the bandage. And that is exactly what Steven and his team at 3M went ahead to design. Today, the solution, Tegaderm IV dressings, is used by medical professionals around the globe solving a problem they had endured on a daily basis for many years.

Design thinking is not about addressing what people want but rather what they need.

2. Focus on the Problems

Just like the opportunity identification frame we presented in Chapter 1, design thinking also focuses on the problems you are aiming to solve. The process stresses on the importance of exploring problems at a greater depth, rather than jumping to conclusions prematurely.

Take for instance, this statement that parents may make about their child: "Johnny's grades are slipping. How do we get him to study harder?" The fact that Johnny's grades are slipping is only a symptom of the problem. Yet, the second sentence suggests a premature conclusion about the symptom and assumes that solving this will help Johnny. What the parents failed to consider is that there may be a root cause for the symptom. Johnny's grades may be slipping because of reasons such as learning disabilities, concentration issues, stress, or anxiety and would need an investigation.

Design thinking therefore advocates that you take an exploratory approach to understanding a problem you are trying to tackle. It also recommends experiments to test out possible solutions. Many successful businesses use this approach to solving problems and generating creative solutions.

An example is Airbnb, a disruptive business offering alternate short-term rented accommodation for global travelers. The idea behind Airbnb was conceived by a personal problem the founders faced.[3] Back in 2007, Airbnb founders Brian Chesky and Joe Gebbia faced a major problem: they could not afford the rent on their San Francisco apartment. To make ends meet, they decided to convert their loft into a lodging space.

Chesky and Gebbia knew that a design conference was coming to town and realized that there would be a surge in demand for short-term accommodation since hotels were expensive and in short

---

[3] Teixeira, Thales S., and Morgan Brown. "Airbnb, Etsy, Uber: Acquiring the First Thousand Customers." Harvard Business School Case 516-094, May 2016. (Revised January 2018.)

supply. Equipped with this knowledge, they went on to set up a simple website with pictures of their loft, three airbeds and a promise of home cooked breakfast.

The site succeeded in securing its first three renters at $80 and generated interest amongst a community of travelers from places as distant as Buenos Aires, London, and Japan. Before they even realized it, Chesky and Gebbia were on a historic journey. As Gebbia explains it, *"Ultimately while solving our own problem, we were solving someone else's problem too."* The simple principle of universality of problems and the global utility in solving them is powerful enough to jump start novel businesses from scratch.

Another famous example is Uber[4] whose initial idea came to co-founder Travis Kalanick from the problems faced by taxi commuters in the city of New York. New York was plagued by an acute shortage of taxis at the time. The problems rampant in New York included poor cab infrastructure such as dirty cabs, cabs not equipped with credit card machine, unsatisfactory service, cabs not arriving on time, and the hassle of having to bargain at the end of the ride. This along with a host of other problems faced by taxi customers gave rise to the idea of setting up a platform to match drivers with customers who needed rides. The fact that the above were real problems faced by millions of users all over the world made the business idea attractive from inception.

The immensely successful Alibaba originated from a personal problem faced by Jack Ma while he was traveling abroad. While stationed in the US, Ma was searching for information online on Chinese companies. However, he was frustrated to find out that he could not obtain any useful information on the Internet. Ma learned that the only means of access to Chinses firms from outside of China was through signing up for the expensive Canton Fair that allowed access to foreign buyers. The idea behind Alibaba originated from this problem that Ma faced.

India based Fitpass launched their fitness and lifestyle brand after they studied the problems faced by Indian consumers who

---

[4]Teixeira, Thales S., and Morgan Brown. "Airbnb, Etsy, Uber: Acquiring the First Thousand Customers." Harvard Business School Case 516-094, May 2016. (Revised January 2018.)

signed up for gym memberships. The founders, Arushi and Akshay Verma, discovered that the fitness sector in India had high market potential and yet low penetration rates as compared to developed and developing countries. The problems including inflexible annual membership structures, limited access to fitness facilities, and inflexible workout schedules had an adverse effect on gym membership take ups. Additionally, the lock-in created by long-term contracts provided limited way out for the consumers who signed up for these memberships. Available fitness services also suffered from the problem of lack of standardization.

Based on an understanding of user pain points, Fitpass launched a solution to provide universal access to gyms and fitness studios through a subscription-based app. They signed up a network of gyms and fitness studios and provided their members access to this large network of facilities. This in turn offered the customers with flexibility in the use of gym facilities. Through the use of technology, they made fitness affordable, accessible, and enjoyable to the Indian consumers.

> *Problems are the focal point of design thinking. Taking the time to explore the problem statement before defining the problem that should be pursued is an important first step in the successful completion of this process.*

3. Principles of Design Thinking

While design thinking is a process advocating for problem-solving through understanding, defining the problem, and generating solutions, it is also fundamentally about developing a design mindset.

The following are the basic principles on which design thinking operates.

Human Centricity

The first rule is to focus on user experience. This is called the "human-centered rule". This is also the reason why design thinking invariably includes an empathy study where you are encouraged to put yourself in the shoes of the users to understand their needs, not only functionally but also emotionally. This expands the scope of understanding needs to include the personal aspects of the user. Do note, however, that the focus is on understanding the user, not how the user may use your products, services, and solutions. What this means is that you have to keep an open mind to the fact that your existing products and services may not be exactly suited to the needs of the users in their current form.

Bias Towards Action

Design thinking has a clear bias towards action and therefore designers are encouraged to engage in a series of actions. This includes talking to and observing users to gain an understanding of the real world setting in which they operate, brainstorming and sharing insights about the users and their pain points with the team, engaging with a wide range of stakeholders to co-create solutions, and developing prototypes to test potential solutions. In principle, design thinking advocates "show rather than tell" where possible. For example, a paper prototype or a model would be used to share a suggested solution idea with the users instead of merely describing it. This suggests a clear orientation towards taking action and adopting certain behaviors that can help to develop your ideas.

Radical Collaboration

Design thinking is inherently a team activity, as it necessitates gathering diverse perspectives from multiple stakeholders. This is based on research that highlights the importance of diversity in teams and varied perspectives for innovation (Auh and Menguc, 2005; Sethi, Smith, and Park, 2001). Integrating the views of multiple stakeholders as well as allowing conflicting views and diverse perspectives has been found to promote innovation (Talke, Salomo, and Rost, 2010). One view of innovation is that it facilitates connecting unrelated knowledge elements to create new knowledge. Diverse nonhomogeneous teams are in a better position to make such connections (Schumpeter, 1982).

Tolerance for Ambiguity

An iterative nature of the design thinking process means that ambiguity is built into it. The process acknowledges that it is unusual for designers to get to a solution right up front and that is just fine. There is a great deal to learn from mistakes and design thinking leverages on this learning.

The most cited example is Apple corporation. The company is renowned for their designs yet has had a string of failed products such as the Newton tablet. The Newton tablet was one of the first personal digital assistants (PDAs) and featured handwriting recognition. Although innovative, a variety of factors including its high price and technological problems led to the product faring poorly in the market and subsequently being discontinued. Yet, the key thing to note here is that Apple's failures are tolerated as part of their cost of innovation and that there is a significant amount of learning attributed to these.

Despite its relatively short life, Newton still exists in the devices we use today. For one, the product pioneered the thought about taking the computer out of the office. The concept behind the first smartphone, Siri, and Google Voice search were all contributions of Newton.[5]

At General Electric Company (GE), the top management pays a lot of attention to their learning through mistakes made in the iterative design process. In the words of Greg Petroff, CEO of GE Software:

> *"GE is moving away from a model of exhaustive product requirements. Teams learn what to do in the process of doing it, iterating, and pivoting. Employees in every aspect of the business must realize that they can take social risks putting forth half-baked ideas, for instance without losing face or experiencing punitive repercussions."* (Kolko, 2015).

Tolerance for ambiguity and errors is evident in these words.

---

[5] https://www.wired.com/2013/08/remembering-the-apple-newtons-prophetic-failure-and-lasting-ideals/

Improved Solutions vs User Experience

Companies often focus on trying to improve the products, services, and solutions that they provide to the customers using a design thinking approach. However, the emphasis should instead be on customer experience. The first difference is in the perspective you take. In improving your offerings, your firm may be focusing on the firm's point of view; this may be your competitive edge or your key advantages relative to competitors such as use of a cutting-edge technology or cost reduction. However, this need may not necessarily align with the needs of the users.

For example, a hospital may focus on achieving the most optimal medical outcome for the patient. However, the patient may have other priorities — such as timely, quick, and painless treatments. It is thus important to try to understand user priorities as well as the trade-offs in addressing them.

Second, it is important to recognize that you may be only a small part of the solution that meets your customer's needs. Therefore, if you focus on the entire customer journey, you may realize that you need to work with other partners to satisfy various needs of your customer. The key is to look at enhancements from the user's perspective. At the end of it all, "What does she or he want done?" is the fundamental question that provides you with the right cues.

For example, a bank that offers a home loan represents only a small part of the entire property purchase journey of a customer. Recognizing that partners need to be more well-integrated within a single platform, Singapore's largest bank, DBS, offers a Marketplace that partners with property listing sites to provide home financial planning, and options to search for property listings, besides home loan application services. DBS even partnered with utilities providers and renovation services providers to enable buyers to settle into their new homes. This is a good example of a business that recognizes users' needs and enhances customer experience by integrating multiple solutions into its platform.

Process Mindfulness

Despite the ambiguity, there is a set of processes, rules, and principles underlying each process, guiding you throughout the design thinking process. It is this systematic approach towards innovation that made IDEO, the leading design consultancy in Silicon Valley, a firm much sought after by large corporations. The distinct phases in IDEO's design thinking approach are described below.

4. Phases in Design Thinking

The systematic approach towards design thinking involves four main phases: (1) Empathy study; (2) Insights generation; (3) Ideation of solutions; (4) Prototyping and testing.

Conducting an Empathy Study

This first phase is probably the most important in design thinking. This step focuses on gaining an understanding of the problem and the needs of the relevant stakeholders.

Observations and interviews are the two major tools used for gathering data that would help at this stage. These are used to understand the user, their needs, problems, pain points, and priorities. A qualitative and ethnographic approach is recommended as you explore the problem to identify what the user really needs.

Henry Ford once noted, *"If I had asked people what they wanted, they would have said faster horses."* It is important to remember that in the empathy phase, you are not trying to simply rely on what the users say they need. You should also not expect users to give you the answers to what you may be looking for, verbatim. Rather, it is about trying to gain a thorough understanding of the users and their context through your conversations with them so that you are in a better position to gain insights.

Generating Insights

Many pieces of information get unearthed as you gather data from diverse stakeholders. It is therefore important for you to synthesize the information and identify the gems or insights from the data you have collected. To do this effectively, you should start by asking some "Why" questions, and dig deeper to find out the motivations or the reasons behind the situation you observe.

Good insights should be authentic — supported by the observations made; revealing — offering a glimpse into how people think and feel; and most importantly, non-obvious — not simply something one would immediately think of.

> *Insights should be authentic, revealing, and non-obvious.*

Ideating Possible Solutions

When problems have been understood and defined, the next logical step is to move on to possible solutions. Ideation techniques can be used to generate all possible solutions from which a short-list of viable options can be developed. It is worthwhile noting some of IDEO's rules for ideation. These include:

Go for quantity — The key rule is to develop as many ideas as you can. Remember there is no such thing as a bad idea.

Encourage wild ideas — This facilitates divergent thinking. The reason why developing viable and non-viable ideas is encouraged is to ensure divergent thinking. Even when the ideas themselves may not be viable, these can trigger thoughts along entirely new lines which may not open up otherwise.

Defer judgement — It is important not to judge the ideas as viable or not as they are being brought up during ideation. This helps to keep an open mind towards all ideas generated at this stage.

Build on others' ideas — It is important for everyone in the team to individually think up ideas. Nevertheless, one of the key pointers is to build on another's idea to derive a highly creative solution.

Prototyping and Testing

The stage that follows ideation is called prototyping where the design team implements ideas in a tangible form using any material or medium. The objective is to refine and validate the design ideas to identify the most workable one. As the saying goes "a picture is worth a thousand words" and a prototype, worth a thousand pictures.

Experiments are a way of testing the prototype developed. For this to be effective, the team needs to ensure that the questions they want answered are clear and testable with the prototype in its present form. Testing needs to cover different target users who may be using it. The key objective is to identify areas for improvement through the feedback obtained and iteratively refine the design.

5. The Good Kitchen

The Good Kitchen case, excerpted from Liedtka *et al.* (2013), is an example that illustrates the importance of empathy in developing user insights to address the right set of problems.

An estimated 60 percent of Denmark's seniors in assisted living facilities or residential care units have been reported to suffer from poor nutrition. As a result, they suffer from health problems and generally have a low quality of life. Danish municipalities deliver subsidized meals to these seniors most of whom suffer from a reduced ability to function due to illness, age, or other conditions. The challenge was to address the daily nutritional needs of these senior citizens on their sponsored meal programs.

(*Continued*)

(Continued)

The municipality of Holstebro attempted to solve this problem in collaboration with Danish innovation and design agency, Hatch & Bloom. At the onset, both the Holstebro officials and the leaders of Holstebro's meal preparation and delivery organization, Hospitable Food Service, defined the problem as a simple and straightforward one: The need to update the existing "Menu". However, this perception soon changed to the "design of a whole new meal service that offered higher quality as well as flexibility and choice to the seniors".

This reframing was possible because of a user-centered design approach adopted by the agency.

The design team began by delving into the seniors' behaviors, needs, and wishes, using an ethnographic approach that included observing and interviewing them in real-life situations. They took rides with food delivery employees accompanying them into the homes and watching the seniors as they prepared the food, set the table, and ate the meal. In addition to existing customers, the team also studied those who had discontinued the service besides potential clients who might soon qualify for the meal plan.

The other stakeholders including the supervisor of the kitchen and the kitchen workers who prepared the meals were also interviewed and observed in their natural environments to understand their needs and work processes. With this dual focus on stakeholders on either side, the people receiving the food as well as those preparing the food, the team managed to unearth interesting insights.

Soon the team found out that the public perception of the workers in the kitchen was wrong. They were viewed as "lesser chefs". The kitchen staff had the necessary skills but were frustrated that they were not empowered to do what they loved. Due to operational and economic constraints, they were forced to prepare the same food throughout the month. The seniors experienced multiple problems: In addition to the loss of control

(*Continued*)

on their food choices, there was the feeling of disconnect and the social stigma attached to having to go under government subsidy. Besides there was the loneliness factor, the fact that they had to eat alone and that reminded them that their family was not around.

Through a series of co-creation workshops, the design team solicited a wide range of ideas for developing a new and better meal service. The results from the workshops were used to test prototypes to determine what would be a workable solution. Different combinations and ways of presenting the food were tested once again with current, previous, and potential clients.

The end result was dramatic change including a new menu, new uniforms for staff, a new feedback mechanism as well as new experience for both customers and employees. Employees' images of themselves and the services they provided changed, and this resulted in improved customer satisfaction. Hospitable Food Service was also renamed aptly as The Good Kitchen (Liedtka, King, and Bennett, 2013).

When Hatch & Bloom was first engaged for the project, they were asked to "change the menu". This was a very functional perspective of the problem — as seniors' nutritional needs were not met, it was natural to assume that the problem lay with the menu. The empathy study, however, revealed that the reason the seniors were not ordering food was because their emotional needs were not being met. The loss of dignity in receiving government-assistance bothered them and they did not like the feeling of loneliness as they ate alone.

These deep-seated emotions were the root cause of the seniors' dissatisfaction with their meals. These insights made the team realize that simply changing the menu without addressing the emotional needs would not solve the problem. The team also recognized that they needed to consider the needs of the kitchen staff who prepare the meals. This illustrates the importance of exploring the perspectives of various stakeholders to understand their needs and the root cause of the problem.

Secondly, the team used a co-creation workshop for ideation where they brought together a wider group of stakeholders with whom they shared and discussed the insights gained from the empathy study. This in turn allowed them to tap into the perspectives of a larger group of stakeholders and enabled them to expand their initial pool of ideas. Furthermore, engaging a larger group of stakeholders and allowing them an opportunity to understand the deeper emotional needs of the seniors and kitchen staff helped the team instill a sense of ownership within this group. This underlines the design thinking principle that the process of engaging stakeholders in conversation may be just as important as the ideas the conversation generates.

Third, the solution ultimately designed by Hatch & Bloom had interesting features. The solution involved not only the change of menu, but also a series of smaller initiatives, such as new uniforms for staff and a new feedback mechanism to facilitate communication between the seniors and kitchen staff.

While these initiatives may seem trivial, they addressed the emotional needs of both the seniors and kitchen staff. The measures helped improve the morale of the kitchen staff and made their jobs more meaningful. They also helped forge a healthy relationship between the seniors and kitchen staff, which resulted in the seniors feeling like they were receiving food cooked with love by friends, rather than left destitute at the mercy of government aid.

In summary, The Good Kitchen case illustrates the multifaceted benefits of adopting design thinking in solving a problem through developing a deeper understanding of user needs and the context.

Chapter 4

Creating Opportunities Through Resource Combination & Bricolage

"Opportunities don't happen. You create them." — *Chris Grosser*

Chapters 1–3 describe how opportunities can be discovered if you are tuned in to the surrounding environment. This characterizes the entrepreneurial journey as one of discovery. In this school of thought, opportunities arise due to a variety of factors such as shifting trends in consumer preferences, changes in technology, or other shifts in the industry (Kirzner, 1973). Accordingly, opportunities would *"exist as real and objective phenomena, independent of the actions or perceptions of entrepreneurs, just waiting to be discovered and exploited"* (Alvarez and Barney, 2007, p. 13). An entrepreneur scans the environment and discovers opportunities to introduce new products or services. However, success depends on whether you are cognitively alert to recognize these opportunities.

In this section, we present a different perspective to opportunity identification: One that emphasizes that business opportunities are to be created rather than discovered. This perspective of entrepreneurship suggests that *"entrepreneurial opportunities are not like mountains, just waiting to be discovered and exploited"*; rather, they are created by entrepreneurs (Alvarez and Barney, 2007, p. 9). In other words, you have to build the mountains to climb. While the two views appear to be contrasting, it probably makes the most sense to think of opportunity discovery and opportunity creation as complementary perspectives since using one or the other depends on the situation. In this chapter, we explore approaches that you can take to create potential business opportunities.

In our research, we have identified ways in which entrepreneurs "recombine resources in new ways" to create opportunities. We name this as resource combination or bricolage and define it as *"making do by applying combinations of the resources at hand to new problems and opportunities"* (Senyard *et al.*, 2014). Bricolage uncovers new resources to help solve your problems.

1. Combining Existing Resources in New Ways

At the end of World War II in 1945, L.S. "Sam" Shoen had just been discharged from the US Navy. Sam and his wife tried in vain to rent a utility trailer for a one-way move from Los Angeles to Portland. Recognizing this prevalent need and a potential opportunity, the Shoens spent their $5,000 savings to buy their first fleet of trailers from welding shops and private owners. They established a commission structure with service station managers who let them park the trailers on their premises and agreed to handle all rentals. Instead of spending on advertising, they painted the trailers with the U-Haul Logo and "$2 Per Day" signs, so that the trailers would advertise themselves wherever they went. To overcome capital constraints, U-Haul established a unique financing plan: Individuals could purchase U-Haul trailers and lease the trailer back to the company. This started as a way to obtain financing from friends and family, but it eventually became an established financing plan for all interested individuals.[1]

The U-Haul story is a classic example of how you can use your existing resources by combining them in new ways. Specifically, U-Haul illustrates an approach known as entrepreneurial bricolage,

---

[1] http://www.uhaul.com/About/History.aspx. This story was also highlighted in Sarasvathy (2001).

which involves "making do with whatever is at hand" (Lévi-Strauss, 1968, p. 17). The Shoens only had $5,000 in savings, yet they "made do" with this sum buying their first fleet of trailers from welding shops and private owners. They also saved on advertising substituting this with painting the sides of their trailers. Additionally, they also circumvented their financial constraints through their unique financial plan, by allowing buyers to buy and lease back to the company.

We also see multiple and unique uses of the trailers besides their obvious purpose as products: As advertising medium and collateral for raising capital. Thus, the key thing to remember is that in this approach you are free to interpret your resource environment in a creative and idiosyncratic manner. You can use the same resource in different ways depending on the situation.

There is a certain level of creativity involved in this exercise. Rather than spending time pondering over a situation, wondering whether you can figure out a workable outcome, you adopt a more active approach. You can engage with the problems and see what comes out of this (Baker and Nelson, 2005). In other words, take actions that advance your cause. It might lead you to new resources or provide ideas for new use of your existing resources.

MicroscopeCo, a company we spoke to, had developed versions of a microscope that images the motion of magnetic beads inserted into a specimen. The underlying technology was developed by Ryan and Ron, who were both professors at a local research university. Royce, a recently graduated doctoral student at Ryan's lab, was brought in as a co-founder. Recognizing their lack of business knowledge, Ryan and Royce enrolled in a one-year entrepreneurship course at the business school in the same university. During this time, they were introduced to Dan, the head of the university's venture accelerator, who provided some seed funding for the venture and introduced the team to industry experts.

Through these meetings, the team met Brian, an experienced entrepreneur in the medical diagnostics market with a technical background. Brian soon joined them as a consultant. The team had secured some funding from the accelerator by then. After talking to the team and studying the technology, Brian became interested in the technology and started advising the team on product development. The accelerator also introduced Royce to the Kauffman Foundation, which provided funding for Royce's post-doctoral position, allowing him to spend time on advancing the idea into a product. Ryan explained:

> *"I think by far the biggest impact was meeting Dan... Dan has always been a source of 'oh, meet this person and send materials to this person, and meet this person'."*

This is an example that shows how a start-up obtained financial resources (research grants), human resources (a business expert who evolved from consultant to board member), and organizational resources (legitimacy and connections to potential partners), by consciously pushing through an opportunity presented to them in the course of learning about how to commercialize their product.

When using this strategy of resource recombination and bricolage, you should ask yourself what you can do given what you currently have (Sarasvathy, 2001), rather than making ambitious plans that may not materialize due to resource constraints. In the case of MicroscopeCo, we saw how the founding team decided to leverage their access to an entrepreneurship course to guide them on their next steps and to uncover resources that they do not know about.

There is an ingenious "leveraging" in the above two examples. In the case of U-Haul, rather than developing expensive marketing plans, the Shoens simply leveraged their vans for marketing. Sam also utilized his personal contacts to obtain financing for additional trailers, creating new resources. Later, he established a financing plan where any individual could purchase U-Haul trailers and lease the trailer back to the company. Effectively, he recombined existing resources to secure more trailers that they could rent to customers. In the case of MicroscopeCo, the team used their enrollment in the course to uncover resources that the university could offer them.

Do note that your perceptions about the value of resources will influence how you leverage your existing resources (Barney, Wright, and Ketchen, 2001). Something not seen to be useful for one can be very valuable to another. For example, Sam realized the empty spaces of service stations, which served no real purpose until then, were a resource he could make use of to park the rental trailers.

Resource recombination is a strategy commonly used across start-ups. As these firms face numerous constraints, they have to recombine resources in novel ways to utilize them fully or gain additional ones. The solution that you can generate depends on the resources that you and others are able to gather and the vision that you bring on board. Many variations of this approach were practiced by the entrepreneurs we studied. In the following sections, we provide several tips illustrated with examples.

Avoid Doing it Alone

An early-stage firm may not have the expertise to undertake all tasks required to deliver its offerings to customers. Yet one may be tempted to take on all responsibilities involved, to try to save costs. This can be counterproductive because the ensuing delays, inefficiencies, and quality issues may offset any perceived cost savings. One of the fundamental strategies therefore is to source externally. For this, you need to find external entities with the requisite skills to partner with, so as to ease the burden.

StenoTech, the stenosis monitoring business targeting dialysis patients that we presented in Chapter 1, followed this strategy. At StenoTech, Bob and his team had to handle a pressing challenge: The patient had to have a large needle inserted into one of the blood vessels for dialysis. However, these blood vessels tend to narrow over time and there were only four blood vessels in the human body that could be used for this purpose. Each vessel had a lifespan of four–five years. So, it was important to maximize the use of each blood vessel to lengthen the life of the patient. Identifying emerging complications ahead of time could ensure early interventions. This in turn could extend the life of these blood vessels as well as that of the patients. Faced with this challenge, Bob and his team went on to design, develop, and market a solution that would help monitor and predict degeneration of the blood vessel over time to ensure timely clinical interventions.

The solution involved designing and developing a hardware and software combo. However, Bob and his friends decided to stay rooted in their core strength of design and to outsource or reuse the technological components already available while developing their solution.

As Bob puts it:

> *"... Being design-centric, we tried not to reinvent the wheel. Instead, we try and identify what other technologies are available out there that we can potentially hitch upon. We don't believe in starting from scratch.*
>
> *And that becomes important from a business perspective in terms of shortening the runway. And so, in terms of hardware, we actually borrow(ed) a technology from [a domain] ... an existing technology that has been in use for the longest time. Just that it has not been used in this application before, so it kind of shortened our developmental time, our proof of concept, to within just a few months.*
>
> *So, that forms the hardware portion ... The software is proprietary, more components, more aspects to it. That is what we use to predict the narrowing (of the blood vessel) and the extent. And we're even bringing it one step further by giving the patients that prediction — we can predict that you are likely to require intervention (by such and such a date)."*

For Bob, this strategy meant that they could partner with specialists who could help them build the requisite portfolio of expertise. Mutually beneficial arrangements helped StenoTech meet the design, development, and marketing needs of the stenosis detection device.

Embrace Frugality where Possible

If you have limited resources available, it is important to ask yourself if you can reduce spending while maintaining quality. Andrew, one of the entrepreneurs who took part in our research, ran Asian Enterprises, a trading business importing consumables such as rice and seafood into Singapore from Myanmar.

Andrew holds regular networking events and workshops for firms in the ecosystem to identify opportunities for collaboration and to understand the market. However, instead of booking expensive ballrooms and convention centers for these, Andrew goes for smaller events organized in cheaper venues. He also avoids expensive advertisements preferring to reach out to his target audience through Facebook.

> *"... I would rather do things which are smaller and more direct for people (so that) we can handle and manage (the event). Unless you want to spend a lot of money on endorsements and advertisements, you don't need to do huge events ..."*

Andrew's venture has since expanded into a multi-business, multi-industry business, offering services as diverse as tour organizing, project management, and construction services.

Avoid Reinventing the Wheel

Firms avoid reinventing the wheel by keeping abreast of offerings in the industry. If a solution or technology already exists, the business can re-use the same, rather than design and build an entirely new product from scratch.

In the case of StenoTech, which we discussed earlier in the chapter, we saw elements of this approach. There, the team strategically focused on designing the core product while identifying existing hardware for blood pressure monitoring that could be integrated with their device.

This gave them the advantage of reliability, as they used a well-tested component rather than building a new one. Furthermore, the strategy shortened the time from design to developing proof of concept, accelerating the firm's entry into the market.

Make Small Iterative Advances and Keep Stakeholders Informed

Sometimes you may find yourself in a situation where things cannot move in one domain until advancements are made in another domain. For example, funding from investors is dependent on your ability to sell to customers, but customers do not want to buy your product until they see that you are credibly backed. In such a double-bind situation, one approach is to try to make small, incremental advancements in each domain and make sure you update all stakeholders on the progress made.

WindCo, an aerospace technology firm, is an example of a firm that used this approach to ensure growth. The company develops a technology that lifts up an airborne wind turbine in a helium-filled, inflatable shell to harness the stronger and consistent winds at altitudes of over 1,000 feet. This technology is able to produce low cost, renewable energy that can be sent through a conductive tether. Due to the nature of airborne wind turbines, WindCo faced a dilemma: They needed a working prototype and evidence of customers' interest to pitch to investors but developing a fully functioning prototype required significant investment.

In order to sustain momentum, WindCo decided to develop a limited version prototype to attract customer interest. To leverage the prototype and to generate wider interest, WindCo uploaded a video of the successful demonstration with the stripped-down prototype, which created market buzz in the form of more than 20,000 YouTube views. WindCo subsequently leveraged on that publicity while pitching to potential investors. WindCo carefully combined existing and newly acquired resources and created an interim solution to seek funding sources. One co-founder of WindCo explained:

> *"With a start-up, it's this delicate dance ... We have our prototype. We have customers, and we have investors. And every one of those wants to see the other two as far along as they can to get interested. So, you do this iteration ... whenever we have a new customer who is interested, I tell the investors. If we get a new investor interested, I tell the customer. And when the prototype is further along, we tell everyone."*

Shorten the Product Development Life Cycle

Shortening the "time-to-market" is a critical strategy that would work under resource limitations. This avoids extra costs and ensures that sales revenues start rolling in quickly. This is especially true in the case of IT firms offering, say, in-house developed applications, where the time taken to translate the design to finished product is crucial. The longer it takes to develop, test, revise, and launch the product, the more expenses the firm incurs.

FarmTech, a firm working in the farming sector, offers AI-based tracking solutions to pig farmers. One of these tracking solutions is a radio-frequency identification (RFID)-based smart, tamper-proof ear-tag designed for pig farmers in China. Chinese regulations mandate every pig be tagged by the farm owners. However, the enforcement of this is ridden with problems.

For one, existing RFID tags are unable to detect if the tag is on the pig or in a drawer. One way out of this problem is to have the officials witness the installation process. But given the huge numbers involved (hundreds of million pigs every year) this is an extremely resource-intensive process. This is where the tamper-proof feature of FarmTech's product comes in handy because it is designed to tell if the tag is on the pig or in a drawer without human intervention. This allows regulators to monitor the tags remotely.

The device also provides insurance firms with a unique means to identify each pig on the farm. This, in turn helps the firms to issue personalized insurance to each of the pigs. This is especially beneficial because of the rampant fraudulent practices: Such as insuring only a few of the pigs and using the tag of the insured live pig to claim insurance when an uninsured pig dies.

Despite a product that addressed a need, FarmTech faced several setbacks including low take up rates for the tags and inability to meet deadlines for delivery, initially. They soon learned that setting a target for completing the cycle of systems development might be the most efficient way to push forward. They, therefore, set a time limit at one-month to complete the feasibility study and two-months for prototype development. Additionally, for some reason, if the feasibility study of a product dragged on for over a month, FarmTech decided to drop the product.

This resulted in a reduction of their product life cycle to six-months which in turn enabled the company to iterate rapidly and meet market demands.

2. Transform Goals as You Combine Resources

You may need to transform your goals as you make advancements by combining existing resources. For example, you may gain new insights about how to add value to your customers and this may lead to a goal transformation for the firm.

We saw this happen with WebCo, a start-up developing a software application to visualize text content. The technology helps online communities to brainstorm and exchange ideas and opinions by using a graphical "map" to show patterns, trends, and the most impactful ideas, to "enhance the wisdom of the crowds". WebCo initially planned to develop a turnkey solution for the mass market but switched to launching customized solutions for specific organizations in the short-term. This happened as they attracted interest from clients who were in need of graphical maps for different domains, and as the team learned how they could adapt their system for commercial purposes. WebCo started generating a small amount of revenue after securing their first few customers. With the revenue stream, WebCo decided not to develop a turnkey solution, as they saw themselves adding value in new ways. One co-founder explains:

> *"In a way, we decided to keep it a smaller scale where we support, every now and then, a consulting project or some sort of this spoken implementation of the software but we're not aggressively doing a company as was the plan before."*

Sometimes, the resources created in one venture may be transferred to another, creating new business opportunities and radically new goals. This was seen in the case of EarCo, a company which designed and developed a three-dimensional (3D) ear canal scanning system. EarCo was co-founded by David, a fluid dynamicist in a research university working on experimental fluid mechanics. David had previously co-founded ToothCo, a start-up producing a digital dental impression system, and had successfully sold it. While interacting with executives from major corporations during the founding of ToothCo, David came up with an idea to apply the same technology for 3D ear canal scanning. David recounted:

> *"While we were working at ToothCo, the head of [major corporation] business development unit came in and said, 'You're scanning teeth. Can you scan ear canals?' And I said, 'Why would you want to do that?' And he explained that it's very similar to teeth, in the sense that they would like to create 3D hearing aids that fit in the canal. But we were focused on teeth, so we didn't even want to talk about it (then)."*

Initially, David did not pay much attention to the suggestion since he believed the technology would not work for scanning ears. It was only after David successfully sold ToothCo to a large corporation that he realized he might have the right technology to start another company, this time for scanning of ear canals. He then went on to leverage his network from ToothCo to set up a team of experts to incorporate EarCo and commercialize the technology.

Chapter 5

Exploiting Contingencies and Creating Options

"When life gives you lemons, make lemonade!" — *Elbert Hubbard*

We spoke about the importance of paying attention to your environment and assessing emerging trends in identifying new business opportunities. But it is difficult to predict the future and be prepared with plans ready to roll out based on your prediction. Often, unexpected and uncontrollable external events upset even the most well thought out of business plans. Such unpredictable events with potentially severe consequences are known as the "Black Swan" events (Taleb, 2007). And under such circumstances, you are often left with no choice but to respond and transform yourselves quickly in order to remain competitive.

A typical example of this can be seen in how businesses were forced to realign and change their operations as they combated the global pandemic. How did they manage since the pandemic descended on us? For one, firms reinvented products and services and redefined business processes in a bid to manage the restrictions put in place. Organizations also adopted digital technologies to better reach out to their customers and rethink their business models.

Those who lagged behind in making adjustments had to suffer severe setbacks.

The problem is that it can be difficult to predict the next "Black Swan" event. Furthermore, when pursuing new business opportunities, you may be on an untrodden path. As such, mistakes and missteps are to be expected; yet you are only likely to learn after the mistake is made. In other words, it is difficult to predict eventualities and businesses often struggle to cope as these events unfold.

Through our research, we identified two approaches that entrepreneurs use to give them the flexibility to survive and thrive in an unpredictable environment: (1) Contingency exploitation; and (2) Options generation. Contingency exploitation refers to converting a contingency to an opportunity by leveraging them. In order to do this, you may need to cultivate the capability for "strategic reactiveness": Through observing changes in the environment, making quick adjustments, and willingly trying out various options (Sarasvathy, 2001). Options generation is about developing various fallback options in the face of volatility. While you may not be able to predict the future, you can be prepared for it. By creating different options for yourself, one of them is likely to be viable even when the future unravels in unexpected ways.

We shall elaborate on these two approaches below.

1. Contingency Exploitation

Contingencies are, by definition, chance events that have an impact on the business. You rarely have control over the frequency, intensity, or duration of such events. Still, they may offer a fleeting opportunity even as they present a challenge. Contingencies may arrive in the form of newly uncovered information or serendipitous opportunities. As you learn more about the environment and the problem your business specializes in, including the characteristics of the market, customer needs, and regulatory requirements, you may uncover new opportunities. While negative events can place constraints on your business, successfully exploiting them may enable you to leverage new opportunities.

You can make use of contingencies in a favorable way by creatively imagining possibilities. If we adopt this perspective, contingencies are opportunities to create something novel and should be captured and exploited quickly. How can you do that? Our research sheds some light on this question.

Remain Flexible

A fundamental strategy that can help a business survive a contingency is to remain flexible. For instance, you can make quick adjustments to your business model such as the targeted customer segment. This is well illustrated by CityDoc, an enterprise healthcare platform that provides outpatient healthcare services by linking patients and employees to healthcare providers and insurers.

Co-founded by Glen, a doctor by training, CityDoc aimed to create an end-to-end platform that connected the medical ecosystem seamlessly for the benefit of all stakeholders.

The firm had initially identified doctors as their immediate target market for two reasons: The co-founders' own background and the weight of doctor buy-in. They believed that buy-in from doctors would pull in other stakeholders, which would enable the platform to achieve a critical mass of users.

When the CityDoc team faced unexpected resistance from doctors, they redefined their target market to include insurance companies, corporate clients, and pharmacies. They realized that if they stuck to their original plan and only targeted doctors, they would not be able to bring in the numbers they wanted.

Glen shared:

"Our strategy worked well initially ... But doctors resisted. Corporate sector knows it is a great thing, cos [because] their customers are asking for it, but the doctors resisted because they think it is a threat, and so having to manage that is also a challenge ... Now we are selling to corporates and insurance companies, they are bringing in their customers and policy holders to the platform ... And then we had pharmacies as well."

This example also reinforces the concepts we covered in Chapter 3 — understanding user needs and preferences that help you identify your optimal target users. Ideally, you want to target the segment you bring the most value to.

Remain Agile — Be Responsive to Business Needs

Agility and responsiveness to changing business needs become pre-requisites for organizations if they are to survive in a dynamic business environment. In certain cases, this can also become a key differentiating factor, especially in the early stages of the business as you are gaining a foothold in the market.

In the case of FarmTech, the firm we featured earlier offering AI-based tracking solutions to pig farmers, they figured that speed and flexibility in adapting to the changing needs of the customer is the most important success factor. The firm supplies a wearable designed to be attached to the ear of a breeding swine monitoring the animal so that farm owners can detect early signs of disease. The farmers can then make the necessary arrangements for ensuring timely medical intervention.

Whenever the pig farmers provided feedback about any problems with the device, FarmTech would respond. They did this by incorporating the additional requirements of the customers through iteratively improving the design of the device. To increase the iteration speed, they set up product testing facilities near customer premises. The speed with which they could make improvements became FarmTech's key advantage over their more established competitors.

Makeover of the Business Model

In a bid to reinvent themselves, firms sometimes resort to a complete revamp of their business models, which allows them to regain lost ground or gain new ones. Such revamps often take place when you learn more about the market conditions that you are operating in. This involves identifying the constraints that necessitate adaptation and the resulting opportunities that come up through these pivots.

In the case of FarmTech, the company had initially modeled themselves as a developer and seller of technology-based solutions targeting pig farmers. However, over time they came across several ground realities that forced them to rethink their initial model.

In the course of dealing with the pig farmers, they came to understand that buying sufficient numbers of monitoring devices could be expensive for the farm owners. It was a time when sensor prices were dropping and the Internet and 4G made access and connectivity easier and therefore FarmTech decided to change their fundamental business model.

They then drew up a subscription-based model in which the farmers could get a subscription for a limited time. Farmers could pay a fee to use the tags and monitoring system for a given amount of time instead of buying them at full price. If they were not satisfied, they could discontinue the subscription. This helped the farmers to avoid incurring huge upfront costs and being stuck with something that may be of no use to them. For FarmTech, this enabled them to attract farmers who were initially apprehensive about the cost of buying the tags.

Be Aware of the "Sunk Cost Fallacy"

To effectively leverage on contingencies, we must be willing to make significant changes even if it calls for abandoning a course that we had initially invested in heavily. The concept of "sunk cost fallacy" suggests that individuals are often reluctant to abandon a course of action even when it is clear that doing so would be beneficial. Difficult as it may be, cutting your losses is critical to managing unexpected contingencies you encounter.

One good example is VentilatorInc who made such a decision to leverage a key opportunity. VentilatorInc develops inexpensive, portable ventilators targeting niche markets in developing countries. Originally based in the US, VentilatorInc was well aware of the difficulty of finding private funding sources from within, mostly due to the product's focus on humanitarian causes in emerging markets. While pitching to various groups of investors, the team was introduced to an angel investor from India, who eventually agreed to invest. To seize the opportunity, VentilatorInc decided to close the US office and move all operations to India, despite their initial plan. VentilatorInc's co-founder explains the difficult choice he had to make:

> *"You have to recognize that sometimes you make a big change now in order to give yourself success later on. I think that was the hardest thing that you just got to totally let go of so much. You just have to say, 'Well, yes, I've put a lot of time and whatever the original plan was, it all ended up being, not worthless but call it a learning experience, and, or, sunk cost really'."*

VentilatorInc hired a CEO from Bangalore, India, and changed the target market to small clinics in India, with future plans to expand to Southeast Asian countries.

Piggy Ride on Government Promoted Trends

Governments or designated agencies launch various public awareness campaigns from time to time. For example, government campaigns in Singapore include those encouraging healthy lifestyle changes (e.g., encouraging people to exercise), promoting social norms and behaviors (e.g., encouraging people to be courteous), and educating people on how to manage a pandemic (e.g., encouraging people to stay home). One strategy adopted by firms is to ride on the buzz created by such campaigns. This not only gives them a head start and a clear direction, but also helps businesses save on advertising and promotional costs. Basically, this strategy suggests that your business could exploit the efforts undertaken by other recognized agencies, while supplementing them with your own in-house marketing activities in a clever and prudently crafted strategy.

In the case of Flakes, the local snack retailer we introduced earlier, the company rode on the Singapore Health Promotion Board (HPB) advertisements promoting healthy eating habits amongst Singaporeans as a deliberate strategy. In doing so, the firm went on to time their in-house advertisements for low sugar rolls so that they could take advantage of the awareness already generated by the HPB campaign.

2. Options Generation

Another approach is to build in flexibility by investing in multiple options. By generating options, you create the opportunity to take certain courses of action when the situation is right, but you will not be obligated to do so if that course of action does not fit the situational requirements. You thus preserve future choices such that you could easily exercise relevant ones as and when the situation calls for it.

Generating multiple options means that you may have a mixed set of ideas including some that may not be well developed to be pursued right away but not so weak that they have to be discarded completely. One approach is to keep these ideas as options that you can exercise when environmental factors become favorable or when currently pursued goals do not pan out as expected. Options generation thus becomes a powerful mechanism for you to both plan for the future and actively create opportunities.

In the following sections, we explore how you may go about generating options for your business.

Set Long-Term Options and Short-Term Goals

Sometimes your long-term goal may be very ambitious and hard to achieve in the short-term. This means that it may be necessary to put the initial breakthrough idea on hold and pursue a more achievable short-term goal. Generating options is about retaining the option to pursue the more ambitious breakthrough idea even as you pursue your short-term goal. Sometimes, this may require you to break down the original idea into multiple-staged interim goals that can be achieved gradually. Alternatively, you may neither pursue nor abandon the original idea, but cryopreserve it and wait for the right time to defrost it.

A good example is LaserInc, a US-based start-up that develops laser applications. LaserInc initially relied on research grants from the federal government but doing so required them to focus on applying their technology to the security sector. Their interactions with venture capitalists (VCs), however, told them that security-related products would have a hard time attracting interest. While the team felt that government grants were the most appropriate source of funding at the initial stage, they knew they would need to migrate from research grants to private funding in the near future. Therefore, the team focused on developing their technology for the security market, while simultaneously looking to find applications in the spectroscopy market. One of the co-founders of LaserInc said:

> *"In the earlier phases, we thought that we could get pretty good traction with markets in homeland security and relate it to the government and so on, which made sense. We started working on some possibility of commercial things you would sell to other businesses that don't have defence and security uses."*

This strategy benefited the start-up, because when they needed to pitch to private investors, they were able to show working prototypes for applications in private-sector markets.

Avoid Premature Commitments

Sometimes, creating options also includes avoiding certain actions that would end up limiting your future possibilities. It is important to refrain from actions even if they bring short-term gains yet results in closing off other important options. This is particularly important, as some decisions made early in the venture creation process may close certain doors upfront. Some start-ups explicitly express their reluctance to accepting funding from VCs too early in the commercialization process for fear of diluting the founders' equity and losing control over the development of the start-up.

Others take significant care with decisions on new hires into the management team. There are so many possible directions that a start-up can go that it may not be clear what expertise a new management team would require early in the venture creation process. Bringing in a new management team prematurely may not be a good idea. The danger in doing this is that the firm may be steered in a particular direction before it is clear if that is indeed the most feasible route.

Renew and Reposition

With shifting market dynamics, you may find yourself in a position where your firm needs to renew and reposition to stay relevant. Yet, it may not always be clear what exactly needs to be done. In such a situation, generating multiple options may help. Depending on market response, you can then determine which option is worth pursuing.

One good example of a firm using this approach to renew and reposition themselves is Chia's. Founded in 1935, Chia's is a traditional family-owned food business offering food products such as Chinese wine. Run by fourth generation family entrepreneurs, the firm imports and distributes Chinese wine. The main clients of the firm, besides household consumers, include supermarkets, hotels, restaurants, and minimarts. Apart from importing business, Chia's organized cooking classes led by chefs to generate awareness and interest in using wines for cooking and other daily needs.

Traditionally, Chinese wine has been a product associated with housewives. Being a traditional family business, Chia's was affected by growing competition in the wine trading business. Chia's was constantly finding new ways of reinventing themselves so as to attract non-users, new and younger customers in the age range of 20–30, to try and use their line of products.

They redesigned the wine labels by adopting modern packaging and changing the labels from Chinese to English. Chia's also actively associated themselves with the youth wings of business associations to familiarize their offerings to the younger target market. Furthermore, they spread word about the social uses of Chinese wine and its use in cocktails besides cooking, and even went on to develop cocktail recipes in collaboration with selected bars. They, thus, generated multiple options to target the younger market.

Explore Multiple Applications of a Useful Product or Technology

Another useful way to generate options is to examine if an idea developed within one industry or domain may be transported to another industry or domain. StarTech, a technology incubator firm which positions itself as a broker in start-up networks, adopts such an innovation strategy. The firm systematically explores potential deployment of promising new technologies in a variety of domains through the development and testing of prototypes to identify what works and what does not. The key strategy used is to actively look for a wide range of applications for a new technology or product.

For example, as the firm encounters a new material, it thinks about how a material deployed in a technology domain may be ported over to the healthcare, beauty, and food processing sectors. Their strategy is thus to take novel ideas across multiple domains where possible.

Founder Tom Hadden explained:

> *"If we have an agricultural farm with a new bio-certified natural ingredient, we can always understand the science and translate that to functional ingredient for toothpaste, for skincare, or for gum health. That's how we're always on the lookout for different applications."*

Balance Between Bread-and-Butter Offerings vs Blue Skies Development

Another strategy is to generate options that grow the business while ensuring a steady stream of revenue. This will enable your organization to remain economically viable while reinvesting in newer, riskier projects that can help your organization to avoid stagnation.

Financial stability comes from staying rooted in tried and tested lines of business that work as "cash cows" or proven revenue generators. At the same time, attaining growth is only possible through investing in new ventures, whether it be a new technology or an entirely new line of business. It is important for you to strike a workable balance between mature products and services that generate revenue, and new projects and developments that are untested and yet have potential.

StarTech once again illustrates this as they use such a measured strategy. Founder Thomas Foo shares:

> *"We also need to find ways for sustainable, constant income — like we need to have our bread-and-butter activities, and have our high-value projects that will pay off later ... 60 percent is bread-and-butter and keeps everything constant; and allows you to invest and grow, and take a couple of bets; 40 percent is then high-value add with more high-risk opportunities, and the way I would handle my corporate portfolios would be 60–30–10, which means that 60 percent is your current business, your bread-and-butter business, 30 percent is new, adjacent businesses that just are new and require extension, and 10 percent is upstream blue skies, quite risky — but very high potential."*

3. Continuous Updating of Goals

As you adopt the approaches discussed in Chapters 4 and 5 — recombining resources, exploiting contingencies, and creating options — you will likely find that you need to constantly change your goals in your innovation journey. Opportunity identification consists of iterative processes involving resource recombination, options generation, and contingency exploitation, which helps you to determine how you could pivot and transform your goals.

Resources are critical for organizations in creating interim solutions such as generating prototypes or solving teething issues. The resources and partners that you attract and work with determine what you can do and how your goals could change as you go along.

It is evident that opportunities are not always obvious for the entrepreneur. Sometimes you need to create opportunities when the chance arises. This is done by recombining resources, exploiting contingencies, and generating options. Opportunity exploration is about gradually defining, probing, and finalizing potential opportunities.

In contrast, if you are simply pursuing your innovation without any adaptations, it will be very easy to be stumped by bumps on the road. We encountered an unsuccessful case that illustrates this lack of flexibility in GrapheneInc.

GrapheneInc was in the business of developing graphene-based electrodes for super-capacitors. They had developed a technique that could be used to manufacture graphene at low cost and at scale. The start-up was successful in securing government grants to fund the initial development of the technology. In order to be competitive in the market and justify their higher price, the team needed to prove that their capacitor functioned better than the others in the market. However, the team had no knowledge of capacitors and the co-founders found it difficult to bring in people with the required expertise. The team also needed to raise funds but lacked hands-on experience in pitching to potential investors. While they recognized the need to hire someone with business experience, the rigid requirements imposed — that the candidate must have business experience and a doctoral degree in material science — made it difficult to get the right person.

The team had limited success in seeking funds from venture capitalists, as they faced stiff competition from a large number of competitors. Facing multiple challenges, the team decided to terminate GrapheneInc. The team failed because of their lack of adaptability. Their search for resources was very limited in scope; they looked locally and imposed strict requirements on the type of expertise required. Instead of cultivating options, changing their goals, or searching widely, the team chose to lament their lack of resources and eventually gave up due to the challenges they faced in obtaining funding. Unlike other cases we shared, GrapheneInc did little to generate possible options to exercise further down the road.

Most start-ups we studied met with some resource constraints or unexpected challenges, but the successful start-ups were able to recombine resources, exploit contingencies, and generate options to adapt to the challenges. The unsuccessful start-ups, on the other hand, were often too focused on continuing on a particular path and were unable to spot and exploit contingencies presented to them.

SmartInc has developed an electrically conductive latex-based paint which can be used to melt snow on outdoor surfaces; this presented a better alternative to shoveling. While the research generating the technology was done in a university, Matt, a co-founder of SmartInc, had the opportunity to own the patent after the university returned the intellectual property rights to the inventor. Due to this, Matt had a strong desire to control the start-up equity and was reluctant to dilute it. The team made a conscious decision to bootstrap as much as possible and not seek private funding until SmartInc had solid prototypes and a business model. Matt was offered $300,000 in funding from investors he met through a business competition, but he declined the offer because he believed that SmartInc's technology was not mature enough to take private funding. In order to grow SmartInc without relying on outside investments, Matt and Aaron, the other co-founder, decided to target small scale market demand for simple products, so that SmartInc could start generating revenue to support further research and development. Matt explained:

"All investors want something. They want a stake in your company. My goal is to have the biggest portion of whatever we can without losing it to investors. I don't want to give away a third of my company and I certainly don't want to get down the road and be pushed out of my own business and

lose everything. If I had it my way, I would have no investors ... I would do it all on my own."

Due to the lack of funds, however, both Matt and Aaron continued with their full-time jobs, working on SmartInc as a side project. As a result, both product development and marketing efforts saw slow progress. Two years after the company incorporated, it folded.

The GrapheneInc and SmartInc stories are reminders that you need to continually adapt your goals as you pursue your business opportunity by securing more resources, exploiting contingencies, and making choices based on the options you generate.

Chapter 6

Partnerships and Alliances

"Alone we can do so little; together we can do so much." — *Helen Keller*

As the saying goes, entrepreneurship is rarely a lone journey. Finding suitable partners who are willing to help you is the key to executing your business idea and growing it into a successful enterprise. Yet, this is not an easy job. A number of challenges arise when businesses set out to establish partnerships. It is important to seek out partners who believe in your solution and with whom you can co-create opportunities. Sarasvathi introduced the "patchwork quilt principle",[1] which highlights the importance of seeking out partners who can help and are willing to connect rather than try and persuade those who are reluctant. Needless to say, how your quilt will look or how your business will develop will depend on who buys into your vision and who you attract as partners.

Partners play an important role in helping you to sustain your operations, remain viable, and scale and grow. You may need long-term alliances or short-term partnerships, depending on the business context and requirements. These partners may include

---

[1] https://books.google.com.sg/books?hl=en&lr=&id=Ve0_8nJcOD0C&oi=fnd&pg=PR1&dq=sarasvathy+effectuation&ots=m6EM9nPbJN&sig=0l7aM27xx33ipE1P4YBtydZL9bc#v=onepage&q=sarasvathy%20effectuation&f=false

individuals you share social connections with or stakeholders of the firm such as customers, suppliers, logistics and financing partners, and even competitors. At some stage, your partner network may also include government agencies in charge of ensuring regulatory compliance as well as academic institutions who support research and development.

1. Importance of Partnerships

Partnerships can bring about benefits such as knowledge sharing as well as access to complementary competencies. Cooperating with partners can help you supplement your limited internal resources. Partners also provide access to specialized technologies and competencies not available within the firm which in turn helps both parties achieve economies of scale.

Acquisition of Social Capital

One of the key objectives of building partnerships is to develop your social capital. Social capital refers to the resources embedded in the social connections that you have built over time. An alliance with a long-term supplier may allow you to make use of their warehouse space when you need storage. This is an example of the benefits of the social capital that comes out of a partnership. The greater your social capital, the more resources you may be able to tap on from your social network, which increases your chances of business success. There are three distinct dimensions to social capital as follows:

(1) Structural capital reflects the advantages derived from the structure of your network. For example, it reflects whether you are central in your network. You may be connected to many individuals or may serve as a bridge to individuals who are typically not connected. You may also be connected to highly central individuals, which gives you access to networks that would normally be out of reach. The structure of your network reflects

how influential you are and the extent to which you may be able to access diverse information.

(2) Relational capital refers to the resources that are accessible to you based on the depth of connections you have built. This defines how close your relationships are in terms of trust, respect, and hence determines the extent to which your connections are likely to reciprocate favors you have given them.

(3) Cognitive capital refers to the extent to which you share common goals, have a common mental model and shared schema, as well as a common understanding with your connections, such that they provide resources in meaningful ways when you need them.

Our research suggests that, of the three dimensions of social capital above, the effect of cognitive capital is the most positive and significant for successful partnerships for innovations, especially in small organizations. Ensuring shared goals and strategic understanding of one another is critical for business success.

Take, for instance, the case of Grameen Bank, and its partnership with Danone. Grameen Bank is a Bangladesh based micro financing pioneer whereas Danone is one of the world's leading healthy food manufacturers. The partnership enabled local production and door-to-door distribution of affordable dairy products from a plant set up in Bogra (Yunus, Moingeon, and Lehmann-Ortega, 2010), a commercial hub located in Northern Bangladesh. The factory served families within a 30 km radius that was relatively unserved by others in the dairy sector. The key success factor in this partnership was the unified vision of the two firms: The eradication of poverty and serving underprivileged sectors of the population.

Achieving Synergies

You are likely familiar with the old adage, "Two heads are better than one". Synergy is the result of bringing together two or more entities that ends up achieving something greater than if you were going at it alone. This can be viewed as the combining of perspectives, resources, and skills of a group of people to create something new and far more valuable together. In a synergistic union, the resulting whole is greater than the sum of its individual parts. In our research, we found that the potential for synergy in a partnership has the greatest impact on partnership satisfaction.

Synergies are greater when the partners bring to the table diverse expertise, knowledge, and perspectives. Synergies are particularly strong when partners have complementary strengths and are able to work together effectively to tap on the combined capabilities. As an extended entity, the collaboration will develop the potential to "break new ground, challenge accepted wisdom, and discover innovative solutions to problems" (Lasker, Weiss, and Miller, 2001). Synergistic partnerships ensure greater capacity to respond to problems and have the potential to think and act responsibly (Lasker, Weiss, and Miller, 2001).

An example can be found in Volkswagen's alliance with Ford, its competitor. The alliance was set up for the development of light commercial vehicles such as vans and pickups and was later extended to cover autonomous driving and electric vehicles. The result was that both companies could integrate a third-party self-driving system into their own models independent of each other. New opportunities opened up for both firms in ride-sharing and automated delivery services. Ford also had the opportunity to use the Modular Electric Drive Toolkit (MEB) developed by Volkswagen for a zero-emissions car model scheduled to hit European markets in 2023. Evidently the partnership placed them in a better position to improve their competitiveness and tailor their products to better meet customer needs while leveraging resulting synergies.[2]

---

[2] https://annualreport2020.volkswagenag.com/group-management-report/sustainable-value-enhancement/research-and-development/synergies-and-alliances.html

2. Partnership Selection Strategies

Partner selection is an important process, as a poorly thought-out alliance will impact various aspects of your endeavor to pursue opportunities. Careful selection of partners results in higher levels of satisfaction with partnerships. In our research, we found that partnership satisfaction was highly correlated with firm performance for small firms pursuing innovation.

Selection of partners often depends on your personal preferences, values, and business needs. You can choose and select partners based on task-related or partner-related criteria. The former focuses on operational skills: Aspects that are important to your organization's competitive success. The partner-related criteria, on the other hand, pertains to your partner's ability to cooperate effectively with your organization (Geringer, 1991).

Our research shows that entrepreneurs choose partners due to various reasons, ranging from physical proximity and familiarity to shared values to complementary expertise to strengths and potential for synergies.

Proximity Based

Sometimes, a factor as basic as physical proximity can be the basis for selecting a partner. The partners of Health Monitor, a firm in the health care sector, preferred local partners. The cultural similarity and the proximity to their target market, Southeast Asia, made them feel more comfortable with work arrangements with their Singapore partners. The firm, which designs monitoring devices for kidney patients, however, recognized that they would need to explore options for overseas manufacturing partners as they scale and grow, so as to keep costs low.

Friendship and Trust Based

A common foundation for partnerships is familiarity — when shared history or a personal friendship becomes the basis for a business partnership. This was illustrated in the case of Toh & Martin, a Singapore-based trading business. The firm identifies processed food products from other Southeast Asian countries that can be marketed in Singapore. They also look for opportunities to market Southeast Asian products to overseas markets including Europe, Hong Kong, China, and the US and Middle East.

Toh & Martin started off as a rice noodles maker and has been working with a Canadian distributor for many years. Mr. Toh found that the distributor liked the products and noticed that they have been supportive in promoting the company, believing in their quality. A mutual friendship based on trust was formed, so when they started their trading business, they looked towards this Canadian distributor to form a partnership. The main reason was that the firms had gained confidence in each other's products and services through their shared history. The entrepreneur also admits that most of his business affiliates either started off as friends or were introduced to him by close friends.

Value Based

It is also important to place emphasis on evaluating whether partners share the same values and aspirations as you. In our research, we have seen entrepreneurs prioritizing these factors above other practical considerations such as expertise or economic standing. This was illustrated in the case of Horizon Ventures, a firm offering integrated technological solutions across different sectors leveraging a network of entities with multiple capabilities. The firm preferred to partner with those who shared similar values: Defined as like-mindedness and a willingness to "hit the ground running" and "make things happen". Personal chemistry and perceived shared business cultures and ambitions also have been reported to play an important part in partner selection (Moem *et al.*, 2010).

Based on Complementarity of Skills

You are also likely to seek partnerships with identified entities who have demonstrable strength in an area where you are relatively weak. Digital Guru, a firm operating in the digital content sector, decided to collaborate with a company in the VR space who specializes in interactive internet content and live action: This complemented their own specialization in animation.

A 2010 Norwegian research also cites the complementarity factor in partner selection (Moen *et al.*, 2010). For example, IKT Interactive, a Norwegian firm that was established in 1996, started off with an idea to develop an ERP system that could be distributed to SMEs via the Internet at a much lower cost than existing systems. IKT at the time was pursuing market opportunities in Germany, Belgium, Spain, Australia, Singapore, and Brazil. As they prepared to enter the UK market in 2002, IKT Interactive chose partners who were both subcontractors and co-developers as a deliberate strategy.

Reputation Based

The dominance of a potential partner in a particular area of business or in a geographic market may be a deciding factor for forming a partnership in certain instances. Such partnerships can, however, be a double-edged sword, as dominant partners can be difficult to manage. Additionally, it may not always be worthwhile pursuing a partner who does not believe in the value of your solution however reputed they may be.

Café Delite, a player in the F&B sector offering their unique brand of baked sweets and savories, cites an example of a dominant overseas partner. The latter was a conglomerate with wide presence in the country through their 80 physical locations and had the influence to make things happen quickly on the ground. The wide reach and influence of the partner made them an important strategic partner for the firm, yet at the same time, their dominance required the firm to manage the partnership extremely carefully due to the uneven power dynamics. Nevertheless, partnering with dominant firms in a region enhances the legitimacy of a new business venture.

Norwegian firm Pronto was in the business of interactive television during the early 1990s. The group offers tailored in-room entertainment and information system for hotels, cruise ships, and apartment complexes. Pronto chose their partner using this approach when they entered the UK market. The partner has been in the market for many years and was regarded as a credible and trustworthy business in the UK. According to Pronto, being associated with the partner increased their reputation in the marketplace and gave them the credibility they may not have had on their own (Moem *et al.*, 2010).

Access Based

Often, you seek partners for the purpose of gaining access to buyers, networks of users, or distribution channels. When a business ventures into a new market, you are the new kid in the block. No one really knows you, and you have no significant history there. For this reason, building a network in a new market will take time and resources. In such circumstances, selecting a partner who can provide you with ready access to the requisite networks will be beneficial. It helps your firm circumvent the problem of being unknown in a new market.

In the case of IKT Interactive's entry into the UK, they established partnerships with firms that already had an established customer base within the country. Access to a customer base was an important criterion for partner selection because IKT needed to pass many gatekeepers to reach their intended target market in the UK. If they were doing this alone it would have been difficult to get past the initial hurdles. They also may have lacked the credibility to be taken seriously by their targeted audience at the time of entry. However, with a carefully chosen partner and their network, they circumvented all these challenges to access the market. This increased IKT's probability of securing quick sales facilitating a rapid market entry (Moem *et al.*, 2010).

3. Partnering Models

Once you have identified a potential partner, you may consider using various partnership models to manage the relationship so that you can gain optimal benefits from the association. A partnership model defines approaches towards forming and managing the partnership over time. Each model comes with a different set of expectations and likely outcomes (Tuten and Urban, 2001). A model also suggests a distinct approach towards building cooperation and trust between the partners as well as establishing communication. Additionally, how the relationships between partners may change or evolve over time is also determined by the model.

Informal Model

You may make a conscious decision not to formalize a partnership until a viable model can be worked out. In the case of Billboards Inc, their partnership arrangement was kept strictly informal since the space of interactive content where they operated in was a relatively new one. The business therefore decided that it would be better to identify the best means of working together with the identified partner informally through trial and error before formalizing the relationship. At the same time, having the backing of a partner was important for the firm to ensure credibility and project a certain level of confidence in the market. The informal partnering strategy provided them with this benefit while affording the flexibility they needed to find the best way of structuring the partnership.

Such informal models can subsequently evolve into more formal arrangements as you and your partners build a shared history together. Tan & Co adopted such a model of collaborating, where like-minded partners started small by working on lower budget projects and then evolving together to bigger budget projects. Compatible work culture and shared aspirations are the key focus in this model. This enables the partners to stay action-oriented from the start even when the financial benefits may not be very attractive. The goal is to ensure a willingness to gear up together for bigger and more rewarding work as you move forward.

Flexible Affiliate Model

If you expect that things may change over time, you can consider using a flexible dynamic partnering model. This will help you to tap on different expertise at different points in time without incurring huge permanent costs. Dealmakers is a business-matching firm we studied that helps broker business deals between companies operating in various regions in Asia. They have been trying out different working arrangements for their staff who also double as their partners. They decided on a flexible and dynamic partnering arrangement with their employees when it came to identifying brokering opportunities as it benefitted both parties.

In the words of Mr. Choy, the founder, "We go beyond the government perception of 'flexible work arrangements'." The firm offers their staff or associates a stake in the business and a sense of ownership by encouraging their clients to set up joint ventures with them. Thus, the company is able to tap on a pool of people on a need basis when a brokering opportunity presents with one of their staff, without incurring permanent costs. At the same time, the staff retains the flexibility to work with the firm and others as and when they have the time. If a brokering opportunity arises in the future, the staff has the option to become a shareholder on a profit-sharing basis.

The business adopts a similar flexible approach towards partnership with other businesses where they form a short-term alliance on a project basis. Such a flexible affiliation model may be particularly beneficial in environments where resource requirements vary across projects.

Give-and-Take Model

A mentoring model of partnership was cited by EduTech, a company in the e-learning space that develops and distributes content to a global customer base. The firm works with publishers, learning centers, and institutions and helps these partners develop e-learning content and distribute these on their platform. They also help license this content to other interested learning centers and institutions. The company works on a "give-and-take" principle, with the core philosophy of "giving more than you take". They also ensure that the chosen partner works on the same principle. This results in a mutual mentoring relationship based on equal treatment of each other that lays the foundation for strong working relationship.

Symbiotic Model

Ideally, you will also want to work towards a symbiotic relationship model, where association with your partners results in mutual benefits and a greater outcome. Paradigms, a firm in the hemodialysis sector, developed an academic partnership which gave them access to experts in sound technology on which their product was designed. The academic partner derived benefits from Paradigms though the clinical knowledge they received in the fields of heart and respiratory health. This in turn helped the partner to morph the sound technology and adapt it for deployment in new areas.

In our research, we also saw entrepreneurs leveraging the specialized local knowledge of partners in order to expand their business. In such partnerships, partners often contribute local market knowledge while the focal firm contributes financial resources and specialized services and products. In a similar vein, some of our entrepreneurs leveraged their local market access and knowledge to form partnerships with American and European companies interested in accessing Asian markets.

4. Partnership Trends — Post-COVID-19 Changes

Like all other aspects of a business, partnerships have to adapt as new trends emerge and significant events unfold. The COVID-19 pandemic situation was one that forced businesses to transform and re-evaluate their partnership strategies.

During the pandemic, firms were being forced to look for new partners and sometimes within unfamiliar domains, without the luxury of in-person meetings. Conventional means of serving customers and traditional partnership models fell short in the face of pandemic challenges. New trends have emerged in just about all business processes including partnership selection and management. While some of these trends may be temporary and recede into the background as soon as the pandemic subsides, others may be here to stay.

Resilience in Partnerships

While eliminating redundancy and improving efficiencies has been the goal of supply chain partnerships in the past, the COVID-19 crisis forced companies to rethink this model and reset their priorities. The pandemic brought about disruptions resulting in bottlenecks, delays, and complete stoppage of movement along global value chains. Businesses that were dependent on their tightly streamlined supply chains found it difficult to cope as a result. In its singular focus on efficiency, the supply chains had grown to become inflexible and unable to meet with the challenges posed by disruptions. As a result, resilience emerged as the new goal in partnerships.

Boston Consulting Group recommends a resilient network that achieves flexibility through selective application of redundancy, such as dual sourcing. In dual sourcing, you design your value chain such that you are able to order a critical raw material or component from two sources: Local and overseas (Zhu, 2015). This mitigates the risk of one of the key suppliers failing to meet the requirements unexpectedly. Other approaches include nearshoring, which weans off reliance on global logistics and vertical integration to bring manufacturing of critical components in house.[3]

Nontraditional Partnerships

The pandemic has brought to the forefront the need to understand your customer and the community more deeply. While this may sound like an old philosophy, the catchphrase has taken on a whole new meaning in the pandemic-ridden economic environment where entire social and economic structures are cracking under the unprecedented stress placed on them.

---

[3] https://www.bcg.com/publications/2021/building-resilience-strategies-to-improve-supply-chain-resilience

Firms have been looking to link up with nontraditional partners in order to reach out to their customers and community in more ways than before. Sometimes, firms sought to partner with NGOs and government agencies in a bid to engage in community outreach programs and to maintain visibility. In the course of doing so, they also kept their brand names alive in the community by becoming a part of their everyday life. For example, the airline industry was one of those most badly affected by the pandemic, due to border closures and travel restrictions. In response, Singapore Airlines tried to redeploy their cabin crew to the healthcare sector as "care ambassadors". This provided a good way to engage the community while redeploying slack resources.

Innovation and Fusion Through Partnerships

As the pandemic brought about changes in consumer needs and behaviors, you will need to fall back on the tried-and-true approach of digging deep into what the customers truly want. These insights may necessitate new partnership strategies that cross traditional industry lines. This could be because of the demand for comprehensive and holistic services that may go beyond the company's focus area. Customers have come to expect a range of services from a single provider according to a Deloitte report.[4] In a bid to support this, a firm has to collaborate with unconventional partners.

For example, companies may strive for greater strategic collaboration with the government and social sectors. During the pandemic, HSBC bank expanded its partnership to include a mental health agency.[5] They did this to foster public awareness and offer resources in dealing with the psychological pressures of money-related problems. By focusing on customer needs and teaming up with an unconventional partner — an expert in the mental health space —

---

[4] https://deloitte.wsj.com/articles/fusion-sparks-innovative-new-partnerships-01620241330

[5] https://www.hsbc.com/news-and-media/hsbc-news/hsbc-launches-mental-health-partnership

the bank created an innovative solution that addressed both the financial and mental wellness of their customers.[6]

Sustainable Supplier Selection

Recent attention on sustainable supply chain management (SSCM) has steered many firms towards the adoption of a triple bottom line (TBL) focus. This includes measuring environmental, economic, and social impacts to assess production and supply chain activities. Traditional supplier selection approaches based on price and quality have undergone a major overhaul due to this trend. As a result, environmental and social measures have been incorporated in the selection and sourcing of partners (Ghadimi, Toosi, and Heavy, 2018). Since public and nonprofit actors are more likely to understand socio-ecological systems, collaborating with such entities allows businesses to leverage unique knowledge and skills regarding the management of such systems (Dentoni, Pinkse, and Lubberink, 2021). This shift in focus is becoming a key consideration in partnership formation.

Influencers and Key Opinion Leaders as Partners

COVID-19 has seen an increase in the use of digital technologies. Firms that have been traditionally doing their business from brick-and-mortar shops ventured into ecommerce. The use of digital marketing including social media saw a surge during the period.

One of the most pronounced trends is that of businesses partnering with key opinion leaders (KOLs) and influencers to promote their brands. KOLs are experts in the fields in which they practice and are regarded highly by the audience as credible sources of information. Anything they say is therefore considered carefully by their audience which helps shape public perceptions on special topics. As such, KOLs have a role in domains such as treatments

---

[6] https://deloitte.wsj.com/articles/fusion-sparks-innovative-new-partnerships-01620241330

and interventions, safety protocols, and prevention of diseases.[7] Influencers on the other hand are regular customers of a product or service who are also heavy social media users with a considerable following. They may be celebrities or ordinary users who have managed to pick up a niche following, which the business can leverage to reach and influence a wider audience.

In summary, partnerships are important, and partners need to be identified and managed carefully.

---

[7] https://oxford.universitypressscholarship.com/view/10.1093/acprof:oso/ 9780199689583.001.0001/acprof-9780199689583-chapter-2

Chapter 7

Digital Transformation

"It is not the strongest of the species nor the most intelligent that survives.
It is the one that is the most adaptable to change."
— *Famously attributed to Charles Darwin*

The decade we are living out has been a time of radical change, not only for businesses but for all aspects of human life. The way we work, the way we transact, and the way we go about our day-to-day lives have all undergone a sea change. This has been brought about in part by the exponential growth and advancements in mobile communications and digital technologies. The proliferation of social media and digital payment options has further fueled the trend. More recently, there have been interesting developments in machine learning and artificial intelligence (AI), big data, and analytics. The trend towards interconnected smart gadgets and sensors that make up the Internet of Things (IoT) has also been accelerating.

The global pandemic pushed through a digitally driven transformation that has resulted in the emergence of an entirely new world order. When businesses adopt digital technologies and transform their operations, they create value and present novel experiences to the stakeholders involved (Morakanyane, Grace, and O'reilly, 2017). This process has been termed 'Digital Transformation'.

Businesses large and small have had no choice but to keep up with the technological changes and the changes brought about by major external shocks like the pandemic in order to remain viable. While this appears to be a stressful event for businesses, it also presents opportunities for them. Technological capability is an important aspect of 'looking beyond' as discussed in Chapter 1. As you may remember, in 'looking beyond' entrepreneurs spot opportunities from beyond their immediate environments through tuning into emerging trends. Let us begin by looking at what constitutes digital technologies and their key characteristics that present interesting opportunities.

1. Digital Technologies — What are These?

Digital technologies have been characterized as being made of three distinct yet related elements — digital artifact, digital platform, and digital architecture (Nambisan, 2017). A digital artifact is a digital component, application, or media content that is part of a new product or service, offering a specific functionality or value to the user. It can be either stand-alone software/hardware component on a physical device or a part of a broader portfolio of offerings that operate on a digital platform. Apps on smartphones or any device that integrates home appliances such as smart refrigerators are examples.

A digital platform is a set of shared, common services and architecture that supports and serves complementary offerings, including digital artifacts. For example, Apple's iOS and Google's Android enable apps to run on smartphones. B2C platforms like Uber and ecommerce sites like Amazon and eBay are also examples of digital platforms — they enable businesses to quickly reach out to customers online.

Digital infrastructure, on the other hand, consists of a wide range of technology tools and systems such as cloud computing, data analytics, online communities, social media, and 3D printing that offer the support for communication, collaboration, and computing capabilities (Nambisan, 2017).

There is an implied hierarchy and interdependence linking the three elements. To make the distinction clearer, imagine a person carrying his pocket bus guide (an artifact), traveling on a bus (a platform), along a national highway (the infrastructure). The passenger owns the guide with the data and annotations he made in it and that is meant for his or her personal use. The bus is a shared service owned by a business entity and used by several such passengers. The highway is the infrastructure built and owned by a higher authority and used by several bus companies to transport passengers from point to point. The components of digital technology work more or less in this manner illustrating numerous interlinks. Some parts of the digital technology suite belongs to individual users, some are owned and offered by businesses and yet others developed and controlled by larger conglomerates such as governments or government backed entities. One cannot function without the other and all components need to work together to fulfil the intended functions.

2. Affordances and Characteristics of Digital Technologies

So, what makes digital technologies unique? Digital technologies have certain distinct characteristics which make them effective tools that can enable you to pursue and develop the business opportunities you have identified. Let us examine the four key characteristics afforded by digital technologies that can help you develop business opportunities:

Immersiveness and Personalization

Immersiveness is a feature that allows for the creation or augmentation of user experience with reality. This feature enables the technology to offer personalized experiences to customers. Examples include virtual reality (VR), which provides an immersive experience with the help of VR goggles by replacing your real-world view with a computer-generated reality. Yet another example is augmented reality (AR), which overlays computer-generated content over the real world.[1] For example, visualizations of your room with artifacts and enhancements such as the ones used in virtual meeting software like Zoom are possible due to AR.

Immersive technologies enable businesses to provide a level of engagement not possible before. The example of Gatebox presented below illustrates how a business capitalized on these immersive capabilities. Gatebox Inc is a Japanese technology firm that makes use of digital technologies to provide immersive customer experiences. The product is a hologram glass box called Gatebox that houses an anthropomorphized anime-style girl, named Azuma Hikari.

Unlike other personal assistants such as Alexa and Siri, Azuma Hikari fulfills a more intimate social role (Liu, 2021). Azuma is designed to be a life companion and does more than a regular communication agent, like playing music, turning down the lights, and reporting on the day's weather (White and Galbraith, 2019) and even sharing a meal and engaging in personal social exchanges with the user.

Immersive technologies are the cornerstone of new developments in the metaverse, a virtual-reality space in which users can interact with a computer-generated environment and other users. Metaverse platforms such as Decentraland, Axie Infinity, and Sandbox are gaining attention of the public. These platforms are like virtual cities that sell virtual real estate to users. There is a growing interest in the metaverse, as people are becoming more used to operating in a virtual world since the pandemic.

Yet the metaverse also brings with it a number of concerns. First, a highly immersive experience brought about by the metaverse may cause people to be cut-off from the real world and spending too much time online, causing increasing cases of addiction. Second, there are risks related to privacy and fraud, with such metaverses also supporting economic transactions. Third, the risks in the metaverse may be amplified because it is an unknown, uncharted territory. It is unclear how governments will respond to economic

---

[1] https://www.verizon.com/business/resources/articles/s/delivering-a-personalized-shopping-experience-with-immersive-technology/

frauds reported in these virtual worlds that are not under their purview. While many businesses are beginning to explore opportunities in the metaverse domain, one should tread carefully, as it is an extremely new domain with many risks that are under explored.

Another key feature of technology is that it enables personalization. Personalization is commonly used to provide higher levels of service in a variety of contexts. In retail, for instance, data on prior purchase and browsing habits are used to determine what items would interest a customer. This helps firms upsell offers, make recommendations, and design their promotional bundles.

Online fashion business is one where there has been an increased demand for personalization. A strong desire to express oneself freely and easily is a driving force behind online fashion buying and this has fueled demand for these services amongst the younger generation. The industry was boosted by consumers shopping at home during the COVID-19 pandemic.

In response, fashion players have turned to digital technologies to provide a more personalized shopping experience.[2] In late 2017, the Japanese online business Zozotown launched Zozosuit, a mobile body scanner that takes measurements to make made-to-fit apparel. Zozosuit 2 launched in 2020 is a polka dot bodysuit which helps customers take precise clothing measurements without going into the store (Guha *et al.*, 2021). It uses an accurate and easy-to-use body measuring technology that makes it a potential solution for online fashion retailers grappling with the problem of returns. Although the initial AI-powered Zozosuit was unsuccessful, the promise of such an application to boost retail is evident.

In another example, eobuwie.pl, the Polish online shoe specialist, has been on a project to build a network of foot scanner islands (called "esize.me"), based in shopping malls and physical stores across Europe. Shoppers use these scanners to generate a 3D scan of their feet which is uploaded to their profile on the company's

---

[2] https://www.mckinsey.com/pl/~/media/mckinsey/locations/europe%20 and%20middle%20east/polska/raporty/moda%20na%20e-commerce/mckinsey-report_online-as-the-key-frontline-in-the-european-fashion-market.pdf

site. These are then used to tailor the shoes and provide an improved fit.[3]

Chatbots

Chatbots are an easy-to-build tool that can help organizations leverage digital technologies for personalization. Chatbots are programs designed to behave much like an intelligent personal assistant and perform a variety of tasks on behalf of a human counterpart. For instance, chatbots could undertake searches, play music, and make recommendations based on stored personal preferences of the user. Key features of a chatbot include human touch, personalization, and natural language communication.

Modern day chatbots vary from low to high end depending on the functionalities built in. At the lowest end of the spectrum, chatbot engagements can be predictable and redundant. In contrast, high end chatbots are able to engage in conversations to the extent that it may be hard to differentiate them from a human assistant.

Chatbots are being deployed within diverse domains ranging from entertainment to education. They are used to answer simple user queries, increase user engagement, to promote products and services, and as a means of acquiring customers. Chatbots are also increasingly being used for mental health applications as well as prevention and behavior change applications such as smoking cessation or physical activity interventions.

Most recently, customer service and commercial social media interactions are also being managed by chatbots equipped with human identities and personalities. Chatbots in business are commonly integrated into a messaging app and used for customer service, sales, and marketing. They may also be embedded into a company website to provide customer service.

---

[3] https://www.mckinsey.com/pl/~/media/mckinsey/locations/europe%20and%20middle%20east/polska/raporty/moda%20na%20e-commerce/mckinsey-report_online-as-the-key-frontline-in-the-european-fashion-market.pdf

Benefits of chatbots

Chatbots have been reported to improve customer satisfaction and empower live agents while at the same time lowering support costs by providing a means to increase customer engagement with fewer staff.

Consumer facing small businesses also can realize benefits of chatbots since they are able to provide easy and effective customer interactions 24/7, thereby reducing reliance on manpower to service routine customer enquiries. These virtual assistants are fast, smart, seamless, and personable and help businesses achieve higher levels of customer engagement, conversion, and satisfaction without incurring higher staff costs. This is because Chatbots are easy to set up since there are open tools such as Wit.ai, that helps to build speech interface for an app or a device. Wit enables you to enter samples of what your users might say — utterances — and then goes on to build an app based on these.[4]

> *Given that digital technologies enable immersion and personalization, how might you leverage these characteristics for your organization? Can you develop chatbots for personalization or AR/VR technologies for immersion?*

Intelligent Sensing

Intelligent sensing is the ability of digital technologies to perform functions in response to stimuli from the environment within which the task is performed. This involves detecting the unique characteristics of the external environment and responding to them in an intelligent manner. Besides environmental awareness, the feature also involves learning and adaptation. Thus, an intelligent sensor is able to self-test, self-validate, and self-adapt besides self-identifying. An

---

[4] https://wit.ai/how

intelligent sensor requires specialized hardware called signal conditioning circuitry to monitor and control itself and other appliances.[5]

The Internet of Things

Intelligent sensing can be enabled by Internet of Things (IoT) technologies. IoT may be considered an extension of internet connectivity into devices and everyday things and objects. These objects may include a range of items including common devices and appliances such as cellphones and washing machines on one hand to components of a jet engine and even wearables.

The promise of the IoT is that "anything that can be connected will be connected". In an IoT therefore, you may find links from people to people, people to things, and things to things. The proliferation of IoT wherein sensors blend seamlessly with the environment around us makes information sharing possible in unique ways.

The key element of an IoT is a smart object which has a physical form and a set of associated features such as size, shape, etc. It also possesses a minimal set of communication functionalities, such as the ability to be discovered and accept incoming messages and respond accordingly. Some of these objects may also be able to sense temperature, light, and electromagnetic radiation levels so as to trigger certain actions.

The pervasive presence of a variety of objects such as radio-frequency identification (RFID) tags, sensors, actuators, mobile phones, etc. which are able to interact with each other to reach common goals has fueled the proliferation of IoT. An essential goal is to generate situational awareness and enable machines and human users to make sense of themselves and their surrounding environments.

Effects of the IoT are visible in both working and domestic environments. For instance, IoT fuels the proliferation of smart homes, where the air conditioning or heating is turned on to a desired temperature before you return home, or a friend is allowed access through a remotely controlled lock in case you are not home to let them in.

---

[5] https://www.techopedia.com/definition/31462/intelligent-sensor

Other everyday examples include wearables that help control health parameters, and ensure fitness of wearers through appropriate monitoring and timely intervention. IoT can also bring together several objects such as machinery or vehicles: For instance, an IoT of cars such as a fleet of taxis, could optimize its own operation and maintenance while ensuring the comfort of passengers.

Benefits of IoT

IoT also holds great potential for the retail sector as it creates entirely new ways to connect with customers and supply chain partners. This enhances in-store experiences for the customers. For the supply chain partners, IoT sharing realizes mutual benefits through the ready availability of valuable real time information on customer behavior and buying patterns. Retailers can track consumer trails through a store and use the information to improve store layout and product placements.

IoT can be a great leveler in terms of delivering benefits within both urban and rural geographic contexts. For example, smart farming may be a promising application of IoT in the rural agricultural sector. With smart farming, farmers are able to assess soil moisture and richness, control water usage in irrigation, and customize fertilizer requirements. By using IoT applications to gather data about the health and well-being of the cattle, ranchers can identify sick animals early and pull them out to help prevent widespread infection. With the help of the collected data, farmers can increase poultry production.

IoT is also touted to solve major problems of city life such as pollution, traffic congestion, and shortage of energy supplies. Smart cities, another powerful application of IoT, is capable of providing real time surveillance, automated transportation, efficient energy management systems, water distribution, urban security, and environmental monitoring, thereby improving the comfort and efficiency of city life. For instance, a "Smart Bin" could send alerts to municipal services when it needs to be emptied. Sensors installed and interfaced with web applications, could help citizens find free available parking across the city. Tampering of public systems as well as malfunctions and installation issues in public infrastructure such as electrical systems (Nambisan, 2017) can also be detected by the sensors in an IoT.

The IoT provides a number of new services and business opportunities and helps companies create new value. The interconnected nature of the IoT leads to openness and collaboration across industries and opens up possibilities for the development of complex yet novel business models.

Ultra-Reliable Low-Latency Communication

Ultra-reliable low-latency communication, or URLLC, is touted to be the most promising addition to the upcoming 5G capabilities. This caters to several services that require uninterrupted connections such as factory automation, autonomous driving, the industrial internet, and robotic surgeries.[6] One of the key features of URLLC is low latency. Low latency allows a network to be optimized for processing large amounts of data with minimal delay. The technology is under development and presents possibilities for business opportunity identification.

The Audi use case

Ericsson and Audi have built a robot cell similar to the ones operating in Audi factories over 5G. Here, a robotic arm builds an airbag and a part of the steering wheel. A laser curtain protects the open side of the robot cell. The ultra-low latency and reliability of URLLC ensures that if a factory worker reaches into the cell, the robot can stop instantly, making it safe for personnel to work with the machines. This feature would not have been possible if the firm were using traditional Wi-Fi.[7]

---

[6] https://www.rcrwireless.com/20190107/5g/what-is-urllc
[7] https://www.ericsson.com/en/cases/2020/accelerate-factory-automation-with-5g-urllc

Given that digital technologies enable intelligent sensing, how can such capabilities be tapped upon to better sense and respond to the changing environment? How might you integrate IoT devices, 5G, and other technologies to offer novel products and services?

Ubiquity and Accessibility

Digital technologies are everywhere which makes them easily accessible. This ubiquity is made possible through advancements in telecommunications and data storage facilities. Besides the 24/7 access, an online store you may have visited is also linked with your personal social network, making it almost impossible to separate the two. While this can pose some challenges there are also benefits. For instance, you are able to see what a friend may have liked and recommended from a line of products, and this helps in making your own purchase decisions. Thus, the ubiquity feature has resulted in a melding of business and social systems into one.

There are many benefits resulting from ubiquity and accessibility of digital technologies. This has made our financial transactions effortless and access to healthcare services at the touch of a button. Entire supply chains and logistics networks can be accessed globally courtesy the ubiquity of digital technologies. Geographically distributed teams can instantly meet and DISCUSS business matters to arrive at important decisions without having to travel to a physical meeting place.

Ubiquity of technology allows firms to select from several strategies depending on the nature of the business. A firm could use a classic disintermediation strategy where digital technologies can be brought in to do away with middlemen. Since digital technologies allow firms to sell directly to customers, some firms may find it unnecessary to continue using distributors. They then cut this layer that separates them from dealing directly with customers, thereby avoiding delays in responding to their needs. Examples include travel sites such as Travelocity and Expedia which offer airline tickets and travel related services without the need for an agent.

Firms could also go in the opposite direction and embrace middlemen, strengthening existing ties in a strategy called remediation. Novel intermediaries such as aggregators and comparison services may be used in transactions between businesses and consumers. This is commonly seen in airline and hotel businesses where an intermediary allows for price comparisons, helping consumers make informed decisions.

A third strategy is a conscious building of partnerships and alliances with new or existing players in the domain resulting in a complex web of relationships. Here, firms may enter into alliances not only with supply chain partners but also with competitors, sharing resources and information as well as leveraging on each other's strengths. This is termed network-based mediation. The idea is to not restrict customers or a supplier to a single locked-in provider. In a networked structure, a broad selection is available to the customers and vendors alike. Through the free interaction within this network, each player can work at creating his own niche. Often new business opportunities emerge within such networks (Pandit, Prox, and Baldwin, 2022). B2B exchanges such as Alibaba and Amazon are examples of such a strategy. Such exchanges allow registered sellers to list their products and sell to a registered global customer base. Small businesses can make use of such exchanges to optimize their reach and visibility.

Ubiquity of technologies allows you to overhaul customer experiences (Liu, 2021) through the collection and processing of customer profiles and preferences, buying patterns, and customer touch points. On the backend, processes are transformed through digitization, which simplifies and speeds up the processes as well as saves resources. Exchange of goods and services can become virtual through the use of mobile technologies, and operations can be supported by the instant exchange of data or money (White and Galbraith, 2019).

At the highest-level, entire business models are transformed through digital modification, creating entirely new digital models and digital globalization. Digital technology allows businesses to gain access to global markets with the help of global shared services for finance, HR, manufacturing, and design. This makes them competitive as well as efficient and flexible (Guha *et al.*, 2021).

All of these changes translate into value for the firm: They now have access to newer markets and information that can help fine-tune offerings. They enjoy higher customer satisfaction and retention. Their processes are faster, less resource intensive and, ultimately, reap higher profits.

During the pandemic, several restaurants were forced to close down in-person dining. However, the ubiquity of platforms such as DoorDash and Uber Eats enabled these restaurants to quickly switch to catering take-out orders that enabled them to continue their operations at scale and even gain access to new markets.

The ubiquity of digital infrastructures has also led to the democratization of entrepreneurship. Shared digital infrastructure and platforms ensure the engagement of diverse groups of people in all stages of the entrepreneurial process, from opportunity exploration to concept testing to venture funding and launch. Crowdsourcing and crowdfunding systems allow entrepreneurs to engage with potential customers and investors in acquiring varied resources (i.e., ideas and capital) on a global scale. Additionally, cloud computing, digital marketplaces, and data analytics have made it possible for new ventures to construct and test novel concepts targeting a wider audience without having to incur high costs.

Reconfigurability

Yet another feature of digital technologies is that they offer reconfigurability. Depending on the context, the definition of reconfigurability may vary. Digital technologies tend to be modular — designed to be composed of distinct and relatively self-sufficient units loosely coupled through well-defined interfaces (Pandit, Prox, and Baldwin, 2022). Modular systems are easier to amend and thus can be reconfigured for new functionality without much effort.

Furthermore, modules can be readily recombined to develop systems and objects with new functionalities (Arthur, 2009). For instance, in the context of a supply chain, supporting digital systems can alter its configurations so that it can respond to the new customer requirements (Zidi *et al.*, 2022). This feature allows the design to be altered to support supply and production capacities as well as add functionality to meet new customer requirements in a cost-efficient, responsive, sustainable, and resilient manner.

Uncertain demands and fluctuations always put pressure on supply chains and affect service fulfilment adversely. Additionally, this also affects supply chain costs resulting in costly buffers, lower capacity utilization and stock outs. Given the nature of competition and turbulence in the global market, supply chain reconfigurability is a key feature that increases the flexibility of a system and allows changes to be made easily without having to incur high costs.

A Singapore based SME that distributed and installed manufacturing machinery for clients exploited these capabilities successfully during the pandemic. They found out that the machinery shipped to their clients overseas were left lying on the shop floors during the covid period. This was because their engineers could not travel to the clients' premises to help them with the installation due to the travel restrictions. The company adopted augmented reality glasses, quickly reconfiguring existing technologies. By shipping the glasses to clients, their engineers could see what the local engineers saw and give the clients' engineers detailed instructions to help them install the machinery. This helped both the firm to continue operating and their clients to gain access to valuable advice in the midst of the pandemic.

This example showcases how a firm adapted and reconfigured an existing technology — AR glasses, which were not used by the firm in the past, to quickly adapt to their needs, thus becoming a key tool for them to help provide instructions to their customers for installation of machinery.

3. An Integrative Case — FarmFriend[8]

Technology adoption has traditionally been slow in the farming sector globally. Digitalizing farms therefore can be viewed as a rather

---

[8] Howie Rosen, Steve Ciesinski, Reema Shah, "FarmFriend," HBS Case E 665 (Boston: Harvard Business School Publishing, 2018).

bold experimentation. Nevertheless, an agricultural enterprise can exploit the various characteristics of digital technologies for success as illustrated by the case of FarmFriend.

FarmFriend is a Chinese agricultural firm that boldly introduced various farm initiatives supported by digital technologies in a bid to overhaul farming practices. FarmFriend offers drone services for the spraying of pesticides, fertilizers, and seeds to farmers in China.

China has vast areas of farming land and yet farming activities have been largely performed manually. China also faces an acute labor shortage in the farming sector with an ageing population and emigration of young people to the cities in search of better paying jobs. Assuming that 90 percent of these activities could be mechanized, the market size for drone services was in the ballpark of 70 million RMB (10 billion USD). With 50 percent of the available farmland utilizing drone spraying at the cost of $10 per acre, the business potential in the sector would be huge.

"Reimagining farming" summarized FarmFriend's digitalization efforts as it impacted how the farmers farmed and how farm helpers were trained for work. This in turn had the potential to create major changes not only within the sector but also in the lives of those who lived off agriculture. FarmFriend thus leveraged the ubiquity and reconfigurability of drones, reconfiguring the hardware and embedding artificial intelligence within it.

Secondly, the firm adopted a platform-based strategy to enable them to connect with farmers and scale quickly without incurring high costs. The platform, which is a key element of FarmFriend's digitalization, enabled them to link farmers directly with drone operators and pilots. This enhanced the speed of response and allowed them to deliver high quality service. Both parties benefitted through the reach and speed offered by the platform.

Drone spraying was a revolutionary way of performing key agricultural activities such as controlling pests and fertilizing the land in China. A worker spraying insecticide manually was only able to cover 1 to 1.5 hectares in a single day whereas a specially designed agricultural drone covered 50 to 150 hectares. Besides, the drone service providers charged $10 per acre whereas the manual sprayers charged \$15–20 for the same. The job matching was done by an algorithm on the mobile phone within an hour which provided the pilots with higher frequency of work than before.

Thus, FarmFriend "uberized" farm machinery and moved on to digitalizing farms. Additionally, they used data from weather stations and research centers to feed a digital farm management system.

This helped them build a deep repository of relevant farming data by leveraging the sensing capabilities of digital technologies. The farmers were able to get detailed information about fields to support operational decision making. This addressed the age-old problem of traditional farming — repeating old procedures with little information on what works and what does not. It is common practice in China that as farmers aged and retired from farm work, their children or grandchildren would inherit the farmland. But the new generation of farmers would have no farming knowledge when the ownership came to them. The system thus helped to bridge this knowledge gap of these young generation of farmers.

According to experts, firms need to focus on two things in order to succeed in digital transformation: Reshaping customer value propositions and transforming operations for greater customer interaction and collaboration (Guha *et al.*, 2021). Evidently, the focus on these two complementary activities helped with the success of FarmFriend. Transforming of operations was evident in the use of drones for spraying and the implementation of the platform that linked drone service providers and farmers efficiently. Customer value came from the resultant improvements in productivity as well as increased access to the farming knowledge base.

4. Use of Digital Technologies — Challenges

We have discussed our conceptualization of digital technologies and explained what are some characteristics of digital technologies that may suggest opportunities to leverage digital technologies to pursue various business opportunities in your firm. Indeed, digitalization is not a silver bullet, and digital technologies may not be a core component of all business opportunities. The use of digital technologies can be challenging, as the development process is long, costly, and often involves uncertainty.

For small firms, in particular, whether they can reach customers' satisfactory level of technology maturity/reliability, and the timeline for developing the digital products/services is often difficult to predict. Either software issues such as mobile application bugs or hardware issues such as digital equipment defects will cost extra time and resources to solve.

Furthermore, finding the right talent to develop digital offerings can also be challenging. While it may be possible to rely on partners for product development, you may also need to be aware of potential issues related to collaboration and cooperation. You may also wish to take note of potentially unexpected but impactful changes in technology trajectory and standards. Technology standards for pioneering digital technologies are evolving, increasing the uncertainty in adopting technologies for product development.

It is thus important to be aware of the potential challenges of leveraging digital technologies for innovation, especially for startups and entrepreneurs with limited resources. Nevertheless, it may be useful for you to begin exploring and considering how digital technologies can help your firm to innovate and discover new opportunities.

Chapter 8

Broader Trends and Business Opportunities

"Our approach to economic development must be modern, focused and in tune with the global trends." — *Ibrahim Babangida*

Major trends emerge and impact our everyday lives from time to time. These forces change the way we live and can affect the quality of life we enjoy. Sometimes, these shifts are so powerful that everything realigns to make room for them and allow them to accelerate. The consequence: Such changes penetrate so deep into the different dimensions of societal life that it may make current business models obsolete. They may also present new opportunities for individuals who are tuned in to these new trends.

Often trends impact the economic environment at several levels. These may include socio-economic changes including radical redefinition of societal values, shifts in consumer preferences, and lifestyle changes. Socio-economic trends are patterns that emerge through the interaction and mutual influence of economic activity and social processes. For example, an economic trend such as growing affluence of a segment of society, and new consumption patterns may interact and influence each other giving rise to trends. Let us examine some of these trends.

Socio-economic trends can be driven by demographic changes in a society, as the demography of people often drive their preferences, habits, hobbies, or lifestyle choices. Businesses need to adjust to the changing needs of their customer demographics over the years, capitalizing on the opportunities presented.

One key aspect to pay attention to is the age demographics in your target market. The boundaries of youth and old age have been shifting as longevity is on the rise with healthcare becoming more advanced and accessible. A younger demography would mean an audience that prioritize transparency, openness, collaboration, and sharing. This suggests that firms would benefit from incorporating such attributes into their business.

The increasing interest in Web3.0[1] apps and platforms for instance is partly attributable to a growing frustration over the dominance of large companies like Meta and Google. Many users feel unfairly exploited as these corporations claim ownership and monetize the data generated by them, over which they themselves have no control. Web3.0 apps and platforms are thus seen as a democratic alternative that is decentralized and open. They are also governed by the community which means that the responsibility of data management is rightfully returned to the users. This trend is driven by a greater desire for transparency and openness, as well as a distaste for centralized control.

1. Demographic Changes

Millennials and Gen Zers

People born between 1981 and 1996 are considered to be Millennials, whereas the post-Millennials or Gen Zers are those born after 1996 (Dingli and Seychell, 2015). Millennials and Gen Zers are considered to be the most racially and ethnically diverse adult

---

[1] Web 3.0 is a new iteration of the World Wide Web which incorporates concepts such as decentralization, and blockchain technologies, AI and machine learning for more intelligent and adaptive applications.

generation. They have been depicted as a group with a significant desire for self-expression. They may be described as the "Look at Me" generation, both self confident and self aware with a planned approach to self expression and self portrayal.[2]

Millennials have also been known to adopt unique values: For instance, efficiency is an utmost priority for them. They also indicate a clear shift from the trend of wanting to own material things, preferring to have access to these comforts on a need to basis, and are known to be open to new experiences. Ownership is viewed as a burden rather than a source of pride, and this group prefers to be free of the burden of loan repayments on cars and apartments. They are happy to share Netflix accounts, cook for each other, and act in ways that chaperone community. Resourcefulness is also known to be a key value that Millennials hold to be important.

Naturally, these characteristics of Millennials have been targeted by businesses to ensure success in recent past. Social media applications such as TikTok and Instagram cater to the generation's need for self-expression by allowing the posting of photos, videos, and thoughts on just about anything they may feel passionate about.

Most Millennials entered the workforce during the economic recession which shaped their life choices. Technology as a means to communicate rapidly and constantly is another factor that shaped this generation. While the Millennials came of age during the internet explosion, Gen Zers were born into the proliferation of mobile devices, Wi-Fi, and high-bandwidth cellular service. The Millennials adapted to social media, constant connectivity, and on-demand entertainment, but for the Gen Zers these are basics that are largely assumed (Dingli and Seychell, 2015). An estimated 75 percent of the workforce is projected to be made of this segment by 2025 and this is expected to bring about a major shift in purchasing decisions.[3]

---

[2] https://time.com/247/millennials-the-me-me-me-generation/

[3] https://www.forbes.com/sites/forbeslacouncil/2019/03/04/the-sharing-economy-is-still-growing-and-businesses-should-take-note/?sh=52c845a54c33

Digital natives

"Digital Natives" is a term used to describe young people born in the midst of technological gadgets who are comfortable handling the complexity of technology. They are exposed to the continuous flow of digital information and tend to view smart-phones, computers, and the Internet as natural components or even extensions of their lives. They take to technology naturally and constantly look out for ways in which it can be used for connection, entertainment, work, productivity, investments, shopping, or health tracking (Dingli and Seychell, 2015). What may appear like a novelty to the previous generation of "Digital Migrants" is ordinary for the natives.

In the past, we had to go to the store every week to buy groceries. We have since become used to buying groceries online. While in the past delivery used to take a few days, now we have same day delivery, and even 3-hour delivery. In some countries like India, companies such as Zepto and Blinkit offer even 10–15-minute deliveries. Digital natives in India share how their grocery shopping habits have changed because of the availability of such services — they no longer see the need to plan ahead for groceries for the week — why should they if they can obtain free delivery within 10 minutes?

Digital natives are thus getting increasingly used to on-demand services and a seamless customer experience. Queuing at a bank physically for 30 minutes may seem like a significant pain to this generation. Organizations not only need to keep up with rising expectations, but also make their services and products available on online platforms in order to reach this group of target customers.

Influencers and key opinion leaders

As digital natives are used to relying on social media platforms like Instagram Reels, TikTok, Supernova, and Clubhouse as a source of information, organizations are starting to realize the importance of leveraging Key Opinion Leaders (KOL), Key Opinion Customers

(KOC) (Manyika *et al.*, 2016), and Influencers to provide information about their products.

KOLs, KOCs, and Influencers are aspirational figures who emerge into the limelight after receiving attention on social media. They harness a large enough follower base to wield significant influence over consumer decisions. As experts in their domain who possess specialized knowledge, KOLs have the potential to help organizations quickly generate massive brand awareness, yet their interaction with consumers is generally one-way. For example, in pharmaceuticals, patient need is at the center of the business. Firms can provide access to KOLs to review unpublished research and they in turn can inform the community on how a new treatment fulfills an unmet patient need.

KOCs, on the other hand, may have much smaller following than KOLs, but engage in a two-way and peer-like exchange with consumers (Manyika *et al.*, 2016). Often these peer engagements lead to higher conversions and can be exploited for business success. China's video sharing app, Kuaishou, is an example of a company that uses KOCs effectively. In one instance, Kuaishou was entrusted with promoting the sale of shoes with JD.com during the shopping festival. However, some users were not ready to pay for some models that were highly priced. Kuaishou aggregated the KOCs that shared shoe purchases and did live broadcasts sharing their experiences with using the shoes. This helped them acquire many loyal fans and push up their sales.[4]

Amazon uses KOCs in a unique way with Amazon Vine, an invitation-only program. The program selects the most insightful reviewers in the Amazon store to serve as Vine Voices. Potential consumers find their reviews helpful since it helps them to make informed purchase decisions. Vine Voices in turn have the unique opportunity to order items free of charge.[5]

---

[4] https://daxueconsulting.com/koc-marketing-in-china/
[5] https://www.amazon.com/vine/about

Motivating via Gamification

As we have seen, using mobile phones and apps for tasks ranging from shopping to ordering food to transportation to making investment decisions is second nature to digital natives. Equipped with this knowledge, companies and organizations have resorted to using "nudges" to motivate desired behavior patterns through gamification.

In a nutshell, gamification is the use of game design elements in a non-game context (Vallas and Schor, 2020). The trend gained momentum around 2010, when game design elements became increasingly used in products, services, and information systems (Kaine and Josserand, 2019). The idea was that this would positively influence user behavior. Users were expected to become more engaged, contribute more, and enjoy their interactions with what could be considered a serious activity. Sure enough, such experimentations have managed to invoke interesting responses since then.

Nike, for instance, had long identified lack of motivation as the key stumbling block amongst its users, preventing them from sticking to a training routine. Healthy habits were not sustainable for most unless there was a partner or a personal trainer to nudge them along. NikeFuel, their gamified site that measures the athletic performance of over 30 million Nike+ users, was a concept that came out of this realization.[6] NikeFuel is a means of measuring all kinds of activities from a morning workout to an afternoon run to any active movement throughout the day. Athletes across the Nike+ ecosystem measure and improve their performance through products and services using sensors embedded in Nike sports shoes and an Apple iPod or iPhone.

NikeFuel tracks activities and document these on the Nike+ platform which then convert the data into visualizations. Users are able to track their progress, compare their performance with others, and obtain status levels that reflected their athletic potential. They are given badges for achieving milestones that can be shared on social networks and displayed in a virtual trophy cabinet. Nike thus man-

---

[6] https://news.nike.com/news/what-is-nikefuel

aged to transform endurance sports into a "game" (Vallas and Schor, 2020).

Another example is the increasing use of loyalty programs. Loyalty programs have been around for a long, long time. All of us will remember those little cards we carried in our wallets that offered membership and special discounts at shops we frequented, whether a bookstore, coffee shop, or mart. With widespread use of the Internet, the old-style loyalty cards had already got a makeover. In addition to this, gamification has made loyalty programs fun and engaging, especially for retail businesses. An example can be found in Starbucks which currently has one of the most successful rewards programs.

Starbucks customers earn points in the form of Stars with every purchase and gather rewards such as free drinks and food.[7] Gold Members who chalk up 300 Stars are treated to exclusive goodies. The loyalty program has helped Starbucks increase its revenue and grow its membership. Loyal Starbucks members reportedly account for about 40 percent of sales at the company's U.S. stores.[8]

In another interesting example, Sweden's National Society for Road Safety and Volkswagen jointly hosted the Speed Camera Lottery in 2011. The objective was to incentivize motorists to follow road safety rules rather than serve up penalties and fines as deterrents if they violated them. As they abided by the speed limit in a speed-controlled area, car drivers were automatically entered into a lottery. What is more, speeding fines were used to finance the prizes of the lottery. (Vallas and Schor, 2020).

Declining Birth Rates

Another important demographic trend to note is declining birth rates globally, especially in more developed countries. Slower economic growth may follow from declining birth rates. Birth rates fell faster during the pandemic with a dramatic drop in China. In the

---

[7] https://www.starbucks.com.sg/members-benefits
[8] https://www.gamify.com/gamification-blog/7-best-gamification-examples-2021

long run, this trend is expected to have a negative impact on the world's labor force. As it is, 51 countries have been reported to have shrinking working-age populations as compared to just 17 in 2000.[9] This trend will have repercussions on world demographics, including labor market demand and supply as well as changing business requirements.

> *If your customer demographics has changed or if millenials or Gen Zers are amongst your customer base, think about how their values and preferences will demand changes to your business model?*
>
> *How will you modify your products, services, and approach to marketing based on this information?*

2. Changing Attitudes to Work

A recent prominent trend is the shift away from being tied down to a full-time job with one employer in the workforce. This is driven by a desire to gain some autonomy in how an individual can balance work and life, earning a living while enjoying what he/she likes to do. Independent work as such may not be a new concept but is characterized by three defining features: A high degree of autonomy, payment by task, assignment, or sales, and a short-term relationship between worker and client. Thus, unlike in traditional work, independent workers have a high degree of control and flexibility in determining how much and what work they wish to undertake at any given point in time. The decisions are made on criteria such as the rates, timing, and hours of the role as well as the reputation of the employer. Independent earners are paid by the task, assignment, contract, volume of sales, or the time put in. Time not spent working is not compensated. Independent workers perform short-term assignments, such as giving someone a ride, designing a website, treating a patient, or working on a legal case (Manyika *et al.*,

---

[9] https://www.ft.com/content/432d78ee-6163-402e-8950-d961b4b1312b

2016). In that sense, the relationship between the worker and the employer is more transient and individuals trade-off the stability of long-term employment with greater autonomy and control of their own time.

Platform Enabled Gig Work

The digitally enabled economy, also referred to as the platform economy, on-demand economy, or gig economy, has given rise to the need for autonomy and unrestricted access to work opportunities for workers across the world. Ecommerce platforms, service labor platforms for rides, household help, and video streaming are all examples. The platform economy also encompasses social media applications such as Facebook and Instagram and internet service platforms such as Amazon Web Services, which provide the infrastructure on which other companies and platforms operate. (Vallas and Schor, 2020).

Work within the gig economy is known as "gig work" and is characterized by many features. In most cases, these are "task-based" and "electronically mediated jobs" that link those offering services to those requesting them through an online platform or smartphone app. The work itself could be "crowd work" or "work on demand": The former refers to work generally undertaken in a worker's own home and could be "micro-tasks" that "co-ordinate the use of human intelligence to perform tasks which computers are unable to execute" such as Amazon Mechanical Turk. These jobs generally require less training and experience and may include, say, describing or classifying images, editing text, validating user accounts on social media, or transcribing audio clips. (Vallas and Schor, 2020).

Work on demand is work that requires specific professional expertise. This differs from crowd work in that it involves "real-world" rather than virtual tasks. Common examples include point-to-point transport, food delivery, handyman, and cleaning services as well as personal and pet care services. While there is no guaranteed fixed earnings in gig work, an individual's earnings depend on their online reputation. This means that workers often need to engage in multiple occupations and be prepared to work at unconventional times such as weekends and holidays (Kaine and Josserand, 2019).

Such digital platforms enable not only freelancers who are interested in gig work, but also a new class of entrepreneurs. Entrepreneurs starting their own online stores on Taobao Marketplace — a C2C platform connecting consumers to shops owned and operated by individual sellers is an example. Being the most popular ecommerce platform in China, Taobao has successfully attracted a large number of individuals to start their business online. An article in The Economist (2015) noted that Taobao has allowed millions in China to sell goods at low cost, and has "reversed the fortunes of many rural people". Similarly, Pinduoduo — China's largest agriculture platform connecting farmers directly to consumers — aims to help farmers expand their market access and sell their produce online to a bigger pool of buyers, cutting off various intermediaries and middlemen. Such platforms enable a new class of entrepreneurs to gain market access and start businesses online.

Remote Working

Another significant trend affecting not only freelancers and the larger group of workers is the dramatic increase in employees working remotely, as a side-effect of the pandemic.

As the COVID-19 situation worsened globally in 2020, companies adopted a new mode of working by enabling their employees to work from home (WFH). In Singapore, 49 percent of employed residents worked remotely in 2020. Similarly, countries like Belgium, Finland, and other European Union (EU) member states saw more than half of their employed residents working remotely. The prevalence of remote working varied greatly across occupations and industries. As many as 77 percent of employed residents in the information and communications industry worked remotely in 2020 due to the COVID-19 situation. Online tools like Zoom, Teams, and Slack have become essential to these groups of employees as video conferencing replaced physical meetings.[10]

---

[10] https://stats.mom.gov.sg/Pages/Impact-of-COVID-19-Remote-Working-in-Singapore.aspx

Globally, McKinsey reported a 4–5-fold increase in remote work from the pre-pandemic period, which could prompt a big change in the geography of work as individuals and companies shift out of large cities into suburbs and small cities.

Some companies are already planning to shift to flexible workspaces after positive experiences with remote work during the pandemic, a move that will reduce the overall space they need and bring fewer workers into offices each day. A survey of 278 executives by McKinsey in August 2020 found that on average, they planned to reduce office space by 30 percent. Demand for public transportation, downtown restaurants, and retail stores may decline as a result.

Post-pandemic, many organizations are grappling with the right balance to maintain between remote and co-located work. Prior research has long established that working in virtual teams that are not co-located has significant drawbacks (Boh *et al.*, 2007) and increases coordination costs. Distance reduces chances for spontaneous informal talk and can be an impediment to foster a collegial social environment, build common ground, and cultivate organizational commitment. Some work that technically can be done remotely is best done in person. Negotiations, critical business decisions, brainstorming sessions, providing sensitive feedback, and onboarding new employees are examples of activities that may lose some effectiveness when done remotely. While some organizations have decided to continue with remote work, others have decided to bring their employees back to office entirely or for part of the time.

Another important implication is the trend towards hiring remote workers internationally. As organizations realize that they can continue working efficiently with remote work, many are beginning to recognize that they can expand their employee pool globally to hire the best talents more cost-effectively. According to some sources, Asia Pacific has seen a 227 percent increase in hiring remote employees and contractors as of 2022.[11] While this suggests opportunities for employers, it also spells potential threats for employees of developed countries who may find their skills replaced

---

[11] https://www.hcamag.com/asia/specialisation/employment-law/hiring-remote-employees-overseas-hrs-legal-responsibilities/412725

by workers in another country at a cheaper rate. Nevertheless, the use of such international remote workers must be handled with care, as the need for trust and rapport building must be considered.

> *As we see changing attitudes towards work, what opportunities or threats might it spell for you or your organization?*

3. Platform Mediated Trust — Rise of the Sharing Economy

There has been a shift in the mindset from owning to renting on a need basis amongst the younger population. This may be driven by greater willingness to trust strangers and a desire to lower transaction costs, created by digital platforms, as well as the mindset de-emphasizing ownership and a realization that access to assets when required is enough for the convenience desired. The trend also created opportunities for individuals with assets to better monetize and utilize them. As the availability of underutilized assets has grown across the world, people have figured out that sharing some of these idle resources such as an additional home, car, or equipment, can be an economically smart option that relieves the cost burden of ownership while chaperoning sustainability. This is a major shift that has repercussions for businesses big and small.

Remember the video rentals of yesteryears? We have also been long familiar with car rentals and book rentals. These older concepts are given a new lease of life with advancements in telecommunications and internet technologies as well as the proliferation of social networking platforms. The result is the emergence of a sharing economy where the traditional concept of ownership has given way to "sharing" (Puschmann and Alt, 2016). The trend has received unprecedented interest in the past decade with several successful businesses such as Airbnb.

The term "Sharing Economy" was first mentioned in 2008. Other terms often used interchangeably include "collaborative consumption", "gig economy," and "access economy" (Schlagwein,

Schoder, and Spindeldreher, 2020). The sharing economy is defined as the "collaborative consumption made by the activities of sharing, exchanging, and rental of resources without owning the goods" (Schor, 2016). Thus, an ownership transfer is no longer the means of transaction. Sharing with pooling of resources is its hallmark.

The transactions and activities within such an environment could be for profit or nonprofit and P2P (peer-to-peer) or B2P (business-to-peer). While P2P entities earn money by commissions on exchanges and are hence dependent on volumes; the B2P models is more interested in maximizing revenue per transaction (Schor, 2016).

Whatever the model is, the fundamental force driving the sharing economy is the increasing willingness of individuals to trust one another with the resources they are sharing. As noted by Choudary *et al.* (2015), platforms offer several features that help to create platform-mediated trust, such as identifying users, collecting community feedback, codifying and measuring user behaviors on platforms, and providing some sort of financial protection and assurance. As individuals cultivate such platform-mediated trust, they gain a greater willingness to explore sharing more and other types of resources. A new societal norm emerges as a result.

Due to its emphasis on reuse, the sharing economy cuts down on the demand for new goods, potentially contributing towards reduction of their carbon footprint. Because the sharing economy can offer ecological benefits, platforms often claim green credentials. The users of such platforms are also conscious of the ecological impact of the transactions they undertake (Schlagwein, Schoder, and Spindeldreher, 2020). We discuss the business models underlying the sharing economy further in the next chapter.

What does the sharing economy mean for you and your business? Are there opportunities to tap into existing platforms to ride on individuals' openness to share resources?

4. Sustainability Focus

Another key socio-economic trend is the increasing awareness of the risks of climate change, coupled with willingness of the society to transition to a low carbon economy. This trend presents opportunities for firms to partner in this transition in many ways. Firms can design for greater circularity and engage in initiatives such as recycling waste management and energy efficient processes.

The modern enlightened customer is more inclined to make purchasing decisions based on how they would impact the environment. They are also conscious of the ethical concerns surrounding entire production cycles of the goods they purchase, including sourcing and manufacturing. Consequently, there is a trend of increasing demand for green products (de Chiara, 2016).

Clean Label Consciousness

Consumers, especially in industrialized countries, are getting more and more interested in information about the production methods and components of food products. Some production methods are perceived as more "natural" (e.g., conventional agriculture) while some food components are seen as "unhealthy" (e.g., artificial additives) (Vallandingham *et al.*, 2018). This phenomenon, often referred to as the "clean label" trend, has had huge implications for the food industry. For one, firms are now required to declare if certain ingredient is present or if the food has been produced using a more "natural" production method (Vallandingham *et al.*, 2018).

The concept of natural food has become increasingly attractive to a group of customers who are averse to genetically modified labels on packaged food (Asioli *et al.*, 2017). Quality of produce is important to this group of shoppers, who have a preference for "all-natural" products. Consumers are also conscious of the source of raw materials, processing methods, and marketing strategies used (Vallandingham *et al.*, 2018).

Designing for the Circular Economy

A "circular economy" is one which turns goods that are at the end of their service life into resources for others, closing loops in industrial ecosystems and minimizing waste (Stahel, 2016). As opposed to the conventional linear value chain, the "Circular Economy" (CE) focuses on cyclical "closed loops" or minimizing the consumption of virgin materials and energy (Homrich *et al.*, 2018). This shifts emphasis from production to sufficiency and propagates reuse, recycling, and repair before remanufacturing only what cannot be repaired (Stahel, 2016). The goal is a "zero waste economy" in which waste is used as raw material for new products and applications (Mirabella *et al.*, 2014).

As evident in the definition above, in a circular economy, there is an increased emphasis on environmental preservation as compared to the traditional value chain approach. A complete overhaul of the production and consumption processes is therefore imminent. Thus, one of the demands of a circular economy is an entire restructuring of the industry and its policies. New technologies that would make these processes easier and more efficient are also sought after.

Optimized networks between companies and eco-industrial parks have been set up resulting in industrial symbiosis. This allows entities and companies that are traditionally separated, to cooperate in the sharing of resources, contributing to the increase of sustainability benefits (Neves *et al.*, 2021).

Moving towards a circular economy however will also necessitate circular supply chain management (CSCM) through the closing, narrowing, and slowing of loops (Bocken *et al.*, 2016). The design stage of the product lifecycle would need to be reconsidered to allow for disassembly and adaptation for reuse.

Global Trend Towards Bioeconomy

The bioeconomy has emerged as a novel economic paradigm in science, technology, and innovation (STI) policy. The mission is to minimize adverse environmental impacts of economic activities, thereby aiming to achieve important sustainable development goals. The German Bioeconomy Council defines Bioeconomy as "the production and utilization of biological resources to provide products, processes and services in all sectors within the framework of a sustainable economy".[12] The approach is grounded on the use of (1) sustainably produced, renewable natural resources, and (2) bio-based innovations. Evidently, this requires a fundamental redesign of entire industry structures that are resource-efficient and bio-based. For example, alternatives to fossil raw materials, as well as the utilization of renewable resources in industrial processes, can be considered part of this initiative. Bio-based innovation includes bioplastics, biodegradable clothing, and products based on eco-design. The guiding principle of the bioeconomy is economic growth with a holistic and global perspective ensuring wellbeing of the world population, protection of environment and climate as well as animal welfare. Linking economic growth with ecological compatibility is therefore key.

In the bioeconomy, innovations link biological knowledge with technological solutions by utilizing the inherent properties of biogenic raw materials such as their natural cycles, renewability, and adaptability. In doing so, the bioeconomy harbors the potential to provide revolutionary products and processes that will protect natural resources and ensure sustained growth. Alongside the environmental benefits associated with such innovation, the bioeconomy also holds the promise of new economic opportunities. New businesses in rural areas that reduce dependence on imports and strengthen knowledge-based sectors are expected as outcomes of the bioeconomy.

With the world's increasing focus on climate change and environmental sustainability, what are some opportunities for you and your organization?

---

[12] https://biooekonomie.de/en/bioeconomy-germany-background

5. Post-Pandemic Trends

On a global scale, the COVID-19 situation had, at one point, enforced new norms such as masking up, social distancing, temperature scanning, and monitoring check-ins and check-outs. When COVID-19 infections were at their peak, products such as sanitizers, test kits, specialized masks, and cleaning products saw a sudden surge in demand. The pandemic also enforced lifestyle changes such as take-away food and eating in. Such a trend may present opportunities for restaurants and take-away services and food delivery applications.

The global pandemic that has been raging since late 2019 has further ushered in trends out of necessity to safeguard the lives and general health of communities across the world. Besides the additional sanitization and increased hygiene requirements, the disease also necessitated social distancing in public spaces as a precaution against the spread of infection. Workplaces moved to an arrangement where employees were required to work from home (WFH) and businesses depended on digital facilities.

Forbes reports an increased emphasis on mental health and greater adoption of telehealth and wellness applications as a response to COVID-19. Additionally, "conscious consumerism" emerged as a result of the pandemic situation that broke out in late 2019. As a result, consumers are driven beyond price considerations and convenience to deliberating on ecosystem impact and effect on human lives in their purchase decisions of products ranging from cosmetics to clothing to cars.[13]

Inflation and Food and Energy Prices

In the short-term, the confluence of several factors — from the pandemic to the war in Ukraine to global supply shocks — have led to a rise in inflation in many countries, with the average inflation

---

[13] https://www.forbes.com/sites/forbesagencycouncil/2021/09/21/powerful-consumer-trends-to-watch-in-2021/?sh=1504be24a2ed

rate in Asia increasing to 5.3 percent in July 2022 from 3.0 percent in January 2022.[14]

6. Exploiting Trends

Look for Adjacent Opportunities

It is important to exploit not just the immediate business opportunities surrounding the trend but also the adjacent opportunities, be it a potential demand for additional products or associated services.

For established business, adjacent opportunities could be the next big step. The famous example of Nike illustrates how expanding into adjacent businesses can help consolidate the position of the firm. Nike as we know began as an athletic shoemaker which has remained its core business. However, once they consolidated their position there, Nike stepped out to launch their clothing line followed by golfing equipment both of which enjoyed higher margins and further solidified their lead position in the market.[15]

Tune in to Weak Signals

While mega trends are obvious most of the time due to the attention they receive in the media and forums, weak signals are not so evident. Weak signals are small indicators of change that have the potential to gather strength and grow into a formidable trend in the future. They are unstructured information that appear ahead of large changes in the environment and may be embedded in snippets of information shared on social media. These signals are invariably novel and interesting and often question conventional wisdom and established norms.

Capitalizing on opportunities presented by trends requires you to be sensitive to weak signals. If you have an in-built antenna that can tune into these signals, you will be able to identify and potentially capitalize on an evolving trend ahead of others who may only

---

[14] https://www.adb.org/outlook
[15] https://hbr.org/2003/12/growth-outside-the-core

be able to see it after the picture emerges in its entirety. There may be higher risks involved in doing this, yet the returns could be equally rewarding.

Be constantly aware of the trends that are evolving around you and ask yourself what they may mean for you and your business.

Chapter 9

Emerging Business Models

"Have a core concept, but wrap it in a full business model."
— *Scott D. Anthony*

As we discussed in the previous chapter, whatever your core business is, you may find yourself challenged by a shift in trends brought about by a variety of factors. These shifts also give rise to opportunities to rethink your business model, which may require your business to make changes to your products and services, the processes supporting the production and delivery of your offerings, the initial target market, value proposition, and revenue generation options.

You may also need to pay attention to emerging or new business models that inspire new ways of providing value to your customers with the help of technological innovations. These models may demand cross-industry integration in order to address changing customer preferences or an unmet market need and result in entirely new products and services.

1. Business Models

Each of the trends discussed in the earlier chapter brings unique business opportunities. For the first movers and innovators who are inspired to try something new, there may be a chance of huge success. Once a successful model emerges and there is widespread talk about it, followers can easily get on the bandwagon, tweaking and adapting the model to fit their own unique contexts.

Therefore, once you have a business idea, you should start working out an appropriate business model for the venture. A business model is a conceptual representation of a business. In summary, it describes how the firm creates value and monetizes it. It also illustrates the links between the inner workings of a firm and the outside elements, such as its customers and supply partners. A business model is often the starting point of a venture as it helps develop a common shared understanding of the business, its operations, and mechanisms for generating revenue.

This need not be a complete description of everything the firm does. The model is general and depicts the cause–effect relations between the various processes that interact with the key entities in the immediate business environment. Needless to say, a business model should be alterable. This enables entrepreneurs to understand what adjustments can be made to the model to accommodate possible future states of the environment.

Often these models become the focus of key discussions at the beginning stages and should therefore be simple, relevant, and intuitively understandable. At the same time, care must be taken not to oversimplify the complexities involved in the business functions.

Elements of a Business Model

According to Lindgardt *et al.* (2012) of Boston Consulting Group, a business model is comprised of two key elements: The **value proposition** and the **operating model**. Each of the two has three sub-elements as discussed below.

The value proposition provides the answer to the question: what are we offering and to whom? The **target customers, product or service offerings**, and **revenue models** are explained here. It is important that the model offers something unique that is not met by any of the others in the market. For example, the briefly successful Tata Nano, a compact city hatchback manufactured and marketed by Indian automaker Tata Motors was unique in design and ensured it is low cost and low maintenance. The model was targeted at a segment that would otherwise not buy cars in emerging markets in India. It was based on a low-margin and high-volume market (Johnson, Christensen, and Kangermann, 2008) and saw tremendous success since it was the first and only one in that category.

The operating model answers the question: How do we deliver the offerings profitably? The **value chain, cost model**, and **organization** are the sub elements of this component. The **value chain** is concerned with the following questions: How do we deliver on the customer demand? What do we do in house? What do we outsource?

The **cost model** focuses on answering the following question: How do we configure our cost and assets so that we can deliver on the value proposition profitably? **Organization** is concerned with the development of key resources including people. The goal is to ensure sustainability and enhance the competitive advantage of the firm.

In the Nano example, Tata Motors reconceived product design, manufacturing, and distribution. Tata outsourced 85 percent of the Nano's components and decided to use nearly 60 percent fewer vendors than normal. This was an unprecedented move and it reduced their transaction costs (Johnson, Christensen, and Kangermann, 2008). Nano was profitable in the beginning because the company reduced many cost elements and settled for lower-than-standard gross margins (Lindgardt *et al.*, 2012). Tata tried to offset the lower margins by increasing sales volume. They did this through targeting markets that were relatively untapped by automakers in India.

Note: Tata ended production of the Nano due to the low sales by 2018. The failure of the product to catch on was attributed to poor marketing: Consumers feared that the cheaper design meant inferior quality and this perception was not sufficiently addressed during marketing. The team also failed to address the class perception attached to the model of car owned which also led to low take-up. Consumers saw a low-cost design as associated with low social class and nothing was done to correct this view.[1]

Do note that a good product or service does not necessarily translate into a successful business. Even the best of products needs a well thought out business model to be successful. There are several examples that point to this fact in the recent business history. Take for example the iconic Apple iPod: The iPod has been widely acknowledged as a product that revolutionized the music industry and popularized immersive personal music in the early 2000s. While the iPod indeed had a great underlying product design, this was not its key success factor. Rather, it was Apple's business model that did the trick.

Even before its launch, products that did the exact same things as the iPod were available in the market. For example, Rio, a product introduced by a company called Diamond Multimedia in 1998, and Cabo 64, by Best Data in 2000, were predecessors of the iconic iPod that had comparable features: They were both portable and stylish.

The clincher for Apple was the way they made the downloading of digital music easy and convenient through iTunes. Their pricing was inspired by the famous Gillette razor-and-blades model, in which a dependent good is sold at cost and a paired consumable is priced high to generate profit. Apple sold iTunes music at a low margin to lock in purchases of the high-margin iPod. This game-changing business model offered value to consumers through convenience and ensured the historic success of the iPod (Johnson, Christensen, and Kangermann, 2008).

Sharing Economy Business Models

Whether in response to mega trends or weak signals, new business models emerge and disrupt their respective industry sectors from time to time. Disruptive business models challenge established norms and question the basic assumptions on which traditional business models are built. Thus the "Uber" model is considered a disruption to the traditional taxi industry. Traditionally, taxi service companies had to acquire assets to start the business. These firms

---

[1] https://www.businessinsider.com/what-went-wrong-with-tata-motors-nano-2013-6

thus go out and buy the requisite number of cars which are then used to offer taxi services to the public. This was the norm that was challenged by the Uber model. Uber used a two-sided platform to connect people who are looking for rides with people who have rides to offer. Subsequently, multiple versions of Uber in different markets appeared. These include Didi in China, Grab in Singapore, and Gojek in Indonesia.

Sharing economies are typically enabled by multi-sided platforms (MSP), that bring together product, service, and solution providers on one hand, and users seeking such products, services, and solutions, on the other. Platforms require a critical mass of users both on the supply and demand side for them to be successful.

The two features that distinguish an MSP from other similar models are as follows:

(1) Direct interactions — The model enables direct interactions between two or more distinct sides.
(2) Affiliation — Each side is affiliated with the platform.

In "direct interaction" two or more distinct sides retain control over pricing, bundling, marketing, and delivery of the goods or services traded. They also share the responsibility to determine the nature and quality of services offered as well as set the terms and conditions of the transaction. Facebook marketplace where a seller transacts with the user directly is an example.

"Affiliation" means that users on each side consciously make platform-specific investments that are necessary for them to directly interact with each other. This could be in the form of a fixed access fee, committing resources (e.g., time and money on learning how to use or develop applications using APIs). This also entails an opportunity cost such as lock-in through a loyalty program. Amazon affiliate program uses this model to develop a network of businesses with product offerings and consumers.

Another key attribute enabled by such platforms is the convenience of accessing goods and services on demand. This allows customers to access the services as and when they need it and expands the variety of goods available. For example, video streaming has been transformed by platforms such as Netflix which brings together entertainment providers on one side and consumers of entertainment on the other. Netflix uses a long tail business model based on the technological convergence of television and the Internet. As such, shows are aired on demand at the user's convenience as opposed to following a fixed pre-programmed schedule, which goes against the convention followed in the TV broadcast business. The greater accessibility and ubiquity of such platforms also enable entrepreneurs to gain access to markets traditionally considered non-users. This in turn opens up new business opportunities. There are several types of sharing models, which are discussed in detail below.

Sharing idle assets and products

The first sharing model is product service systems, where members share assets or products they own, but are not fully utilizing. This creates an opportunity to share resources that are otherwise sitting idly with others who are in need of them. One good example is Airbnb, which connects people needing short-term stays with homeowners who have space that they are not using. It makes sense for these homeowners to utilize these idle resources by renting them out. Another example is the carsharing service Zipcar that offers an alternative to owning or renting a car through a network of shared, on-demand vehicles.[2]

Another variation of the model called redistribution markets centers on "re-ownership". In this type of sharing, used or pre-owned goods are passed from someone who owns it but does not want it to someone new. The goal is to deal with waste through "reduce, reuse, recycle, and repair".[3] The model uses peer-to-peer matching and social networks to make re-ownership possible. An example of redistribution markets is the online platform

---

[2] https://www.zipcar.com/carsharing
[3] https://wiki.p2pfoundation.net/Redistribution_Markets

NeighborGoods.com which allows for things to be sold within a local market.

Sharing skills and time

People who may not be meaningfully engaged otherwise and those with time to spare may share their skills and time. Food delivery platforms such as Uber Eats and Grab leverage this model. Food delivery personnel who provide the services of picking up food and sending them to the desired destination are hired on a sharing basis. Another example is the skill sharing platform TaskRabbit (taskrab bit.com) (Matzler, Veider, and Katham, 2015). It connects people looking for help with odd jobs and errands with skilled "Taskers"[4] in the locality.

Sharing ideas — crowdsourcing

Crowdsourcing is the IT-mediated engagement of crowds for the purposes of problem-solving, task completion, idea generation, and production (Brabham, 2008). Wisdom of crowds has been a topic of interest since the Grecian days of democracy. The idea that the collective wisdom of a group of people could be greater and more reliable than the wisdom of any one member is the concept underlying the popular Wikipedia.

The term "crowdsourcing" was first coined in 2006 by American journalist Jeff Howe. Howe viewed the process as one where a function is outsourced from internal employees to a large network of people in the form of an open call. This crowd is usually heterogeneous and made up of amateurs, volunteers, experts, and companies. As such, may not belong to a specific community (Estellés-Arolas *et al.*, 2005). Depending on the context, the crowd members could be the source of knowledge, ideas, opinions, or reviews.

---

[4] https://www.taskrabbit.com/about

An example of crowdsourcing can be found in LEGO which established their LEGO Ideas platform in 2012. The platform allows consumers (i.e., the crowd) to submit their ideas for new LEGO sets directly to the company. The consumers vote and offer feedback on ideas submitted which helps the LEGO team identify popular ideas. Any idea that has received over 10,000 votes is reviewed by LEGO and if the idea is selected, the submitter is offered the opportunity to work with the LEGO team to convert their idea into a final product. The submitter also gets royalties on sales. This allows LEGO to generate plenty of creative ideas and assess how these ideas are received by the users. LEGO developed the "Yellow Submarine", "Women of NASA", and "Old Fishing Store" sets using crowdsourcing.[5]

Frito Lay's "Do Us A Flavor" campaign is considered one of the most successful crowdsourcing campaigns. The campaign was first launched in the U.S. in July 2012 with a pop-up store in Times Square showcasing its current 22 Lay's flavors. The company then created a Facebook page for participants to submit ideas for new potato chip flavors. Fans of Lay's could pitch their flavor idea and the story behind it. Three finalist flavors would then be chosen to be fully developed and brought to store. Each flavor would then be voted on nationwide to decide the ultimate winner of the one million grand prize.[6] On submission, users received a generated image of a Lay's bag customized to reflect their submitted flavor, which they could share on their social media platforms.[7] Three flavors emerged from this exercise: Cheesy Garlic Bread, Chicken & Waffles, and Sriracha.

When such models suddenly catapult themselves to unprecedented success, opportunities and lessons unfold. Aspiring

---

[5] https://ideas.lego.com/howitworks

[6] https://www.fritolay.com/news/get-your-pitch-on-lay-s-do-us-a-flavor-seeks-america-s-next-great-potato-chip-flavor-and-celebrates-the-stories-behind-the-flavors-with-1-million-award

[7] https://digital.hbs.edu/platform-digit/submission/crowdsourcing-your-next-chip-flavor-lays-do-us-a-flavor-campaign/

entrepreneurs could capitalize on these opportunities in a follow-the-leader pattern, one of the most common approaches used globally. Often these follower models will emulate one of the above models, but tweak or customize them to address a different sector or geographic market. Such modifications will help them leverage the successful aspects of the tested business model thus minimizing risks, while at the same time incorporating unique features attractive to the audience in the selected markets.

How can you emulate one of these sharing economy models in a new domain?

2. Product-as-a-Service Model

There is also a shift in business models, where organizations move from sale of products to sale of services. This is called a Product-as-a-Service model, where customers pay for a service rather than purchase the product or equipment to get the work done. Thus, instead of buying a lawn mower (product) customers may prefer to get the lawn maintained (service) periodically.

The basic premise of this model is a shift in focus to customer needs and the jobs they need to get done (Christensen, 2016) from merely making and selling products. As Theodore Levitt put it, "People don't want to buy a quarter-inch drill. They want a quarter-inch hole!"[8]

The customer pays a fee for the service consumed, while the ownership of the product remains with the provider, who bears all operational costs. The focus thus moves away from ownership to access to the product. A product sales model tends to focus on creating economies of scale by decreasing the cost of production with a high volume of standardized output. A service model, on the

---

[8] https://hbswk.hbs.edu/item/what-customers-want-from-your-products#:~:text=Customers%20want%20to%20%22hire%22%20a,a%20quarter%2Dinch%20hole!%22

other hand, focuses on offering solutions rather than products. This requires a focus on personalization — understanding the needs of customers and putting together a customized solution to meet those needs.

Product sales models also tend to adopt a one-off transaction with an up-front payment model. In such a model, merchants simply sell the products and have limited follow-ups with customers, beyond the provision of simple warranties and repairs when needed. A service model, on the other hand, adopts a revenue model that may either be subscription-based or pay-per-use. The model may even adopt an outcome-based pricing approach, where users pay based on the outcomes achieved (e.g., paying a percentage of savings obtained).

The product-as-a-service model is not entirely new as a concept: We have had Xerox offering "pay-per-copy" since the early 70s.[9] Such a product-as-a-service model has also been introduced in the mass consumer market. For example, the Nespresso by Nestle uses a machine-and-pod concept for making espresso. Nestle coffee machine is designed with a fitted aluminium coffee pod so that users can get the perfect espresso at the push of a button. The Nespresso coffee capsule innovation thus shifts the focus from products or services per se, to the activities surrounding them.

The model, thus, ties customers directly to Nespresso through a direct sales system that sells the cups that go into the machine. Nestle also outsources production of the coffee machines to third party manufacturers but keeps them to function as part of the distribution channel. The system has been a success as it simplified coffeemaking activity with a selection of flavors emphasizing the enjoyment factor added to high standards of servicing.[10]

Another example can be seen at the Schiphol airport in Amsterdam, where the group has entered into a collaboration with

---

[9] https://www.weforum.org/agenda/2020/11/what-is-servitization-and-how-can-it-help-save-the-planet/

[10] https://empirics.asia/business-model-nespresso/

Cofely and Royal Philips, the global leader in lighting, for the new lighting in their terminal buildings. As per the lighting as a service contract, Schiphol pays for the light it uses, while Philips would remain the owner of all fixtures and installations. Philips and Cofely will be jointly responsible for the performance and maintenance of the lighting system as well as for managing the reuse and recycling of the fixtures at the end of life. While Philips retains ownership of all the equipment, Schiphol Group leases it for the duration of the contract. At the end of the contract, fixtures will be reused elsewhere after necessary upgrades, resulting in resource reduction.

Additionally, the lighting fixtures were designed to last 75 percent longer than conventional fixtures and this improved the serviceability and extended their lives. The fixtures were made in such a way that they could be replaced individually, and this reduced maintenance costs resulting in reduction of raw material consumption.[11] Schiphol thus guarantees their passengers a well-lit, comfortable environment while at the same time meeting their own sustainability goals. In summary, this is a shift from traditional business models to an outcome-based, product-as-a-service (PaaS) model.

As we can see in the Schiphol airport example, the product-as-a-service model also encourages businesses to rethink the long-term implications of their product design, including the energy consumption during operation as well as its impact on the environment — both during operations and in dealing with the end-of-life of the product.

The product-as-a-service model supports design for circularity in that the design takes into consideration how the products should be retired and whether they can be refurbished or reused at the end of its life. It will also encourage organizations to ensure energy efficiency during product use. This model can therefore be a major contributor to de-carbonization efforts globally and accelerate the push towards sustainability.

---

[11] https://www.signify.com/global/our-company/news/press-release-archive/2015/20150416-philips-provides-light-as-a-service-to-schiphol-airport#:~:text=The%20light%20as%20a%20service,recycling%20at%20end%20of%20life.

In another example, tool manufacturer Hilti moved away from selling high-quality tools to selling tool fleet management services to construction companies, after a key customer requested a holistic tool management system to increase their productivity. As a premium brand, Hilti was seeing significant challenges in selling premium tools, with the commoditization of the tools market. With tools becoming cheaper, however, Hilti realized that customers faced a different set of challenges: The tools were no longer well maintained. As a result, customers were faced with problems of mismatched and broken tools, or unavailable tools when they open up their toolbox. This resulted in delays in work schedules and negatively affected work site productivity. As they identified these challenges, Hilti realized that their key role is to help companies manage their tools, rather than simply sell.

They therefore transformed themselves and started to offer tool fleet management services where they deliver tools to the work sites when their customers require them. This shift helped Hilti overcome the global financial crisis of 2008 when the construction industry came to a grinding standstill.[12] Much like the fleet management services in the automotive sector, Hilti offers a full package, including tools, service, and repairs for a fixed monthly fee. The fee also includes theft protection, inventory management, and upgrading to new models.[13]

This model not only helped the companies financially, but also enabled Hilti to manage their tools more sustainably. With fleet management, wastage of tools is reduced, as customers no longer buy tools that they do not need. The more robust repair and maintenance regime Hilti adopted for their tool fleet also ensured that tools have a longer life span. Hilti also got to reuse tools that customers no longer need, reducing wasteful discard of working tools.

---

[12] https://www.strategyzer.com/blog/lessons-from-hilti-on-what-it-takes-to-shift-from-a-product-to-a-service-business-model

[13] https://www.wintersteiger.com/en/Plant-Breeding-and-Research/News/Latest-News/63-Trend-barometer-What-is-servitization

> *If your organization has been selling products, how will a product-as-a-service model benefit your organization?*

3. Monetizing Existing Resources

Assets accumulated but not recognized as such by individuals or organizations can be monetized as a strategy. One example is Google, which helps website owners monetize their website traffic by linking them with advertisers, who can place advertisements on their websites. Websites like Shutterstock and Dreamstime allow photographers to monetize their work by selling their photographs on their websites.

Leveraging Data and Analyses

Another key asset many firms are able to monetize is data. The increasing volume, richness, and variety of data captured and stored on the Internet as well as in organizational systems presents an important asset that many firms may be able to exploit. Data is thus no longer viewed as a passive entity but an active asset that can be leveraged by firms that own it. Data is now a novel source of revenue, and the process of creating wealth from it is called "data monetization". (Hanafizadeh and Harati Nik, 2020).

There are ways to monetize and create value from data by leveraging on the analysis or creating data-based services (Parvinen, 2020). For example, aggregated data captured by smart vehicles could provide insights about customer demographics, vehicle ownership, and usage patterns for the automobile industry, and such analysis can be sold to automobile manufacturers. Several companies also develop and sell data-driven services such as driving style suggestions or fleet management solutions.

Companies can also leverage on aggregated data and the insights derived from these. They could share aggregated or transformed data and analyses to potential businesses. Such resources help buyers to better understand consumers, competitors, production elements, or business environments and to improve decision making.

For example, Vodafone sells anonymized network data to the Dutch digital navigation company TomTom. Vodafone has real time, location-based data about its customers that TomTom is interested in as the leading geolocation technology specialist. TomTom uses driver insights developed from these datasets to design maps used in automated driving and navigation software installed in high-end cars.[14]

Another example is the Finnish pharmaceutical company Tamro. Tamro is the Finnish leader in pharmaceutical distribution and offers a wide range of services to operators in the health and wellbeing industry including solutions for research and innovation. They also provide drug manufacturers and other suppliers with insights into consumer spending on medical and healthcare products sold in their outlets. In addition, Tamro also offers pharmacies information on competitor sales.

A third example is of Barclays that provides SMEs with information on their revenue inflows and outflows as well as analysis of historical payments and transactions. Customers are also able to compare their own data with that from similar businesses in nearby locations.

Selling Data-Based Services

Some companies create new services based on the data collected from users using multi-sided business models, implementing these via digital interfaces such as dashboards. Users pay to use such services.

For instance, Google's smart thermostat Nest provides data on users' energy consumption to electricity utility firms. Nest thermostat shows you how much energy you use every day in Energy History and every month in your Home Report. It also learns what temperature you like and builds a heating/cooling schedule around your

---

[14] https://www.tomtom.com/company/our-story/

own. It can learn your schedule, turn itself down when nobody is home, and balance temperatures around your home to make you comfortable while using less energy.[15] According to studies, this feature saves people an average of 10 percent to 12 percent on heating bills and 15 percent on cooling bills, enabling them to recover its cost in two years. Nest does not share raw data with the utility companies, but it enables them to balance users' energy grid.[16]

Both Google and Facebook provide services that enable customers to target their advertisements at specific user groups (Parvinen, 2020). These companies monetize usage data by offering marketing tools for businesses to extend the reach of their advertisements. When the ad is running, organizations can track performance and edit the campaign. This helps them see if one version of the ad is working better than another and whether the ad is being delivered efficiently.[17]

> *Are there assets in your firm that you can monetize? Are there ways that you may help your customers monetize their assets?*

4. Improving Current Business Models

Rather than radically changing your business model, you could make incremental changes to your current model in various ways as described in the following sections.

Changing Revenue Models

One way is to reconsider the revenue model your firm is using i.e., how you charge customers. Making some tweaks to the revenue model can spell significant opportunities for firms. This can help

---

[15] https://www.nytimes.com/wirecutter/reviews/the-best-thermostat/
[16] https://store.google.com/us/product/nest_learning_thermostat_3rd_gen?hl=en-US
[17] https://www.facebook.com/business/ads

the firms to engage the customers in new ways. Let us look at a few revenue models that have been used by successful businesses.

Unbundling

In a bundled model, companies package different products and offerings together for a flat price. Imagine an auto dealer offering a car with servicing and repairs for the first 20,000 km at a fixed price. The bundled price will be attractive to the customer when considering the total individual costs of the components. In an unbundled model, the company goes in the opposite direction and focuses on offering a core component or service and all other additional services or components as add-ons on an optional basis.

A good example is the comparison of a full-service airline to a budget airline. A full-service airline provides a full suite of services at one price, including transportation of customers from one place to another, luggage check-in services, meal services, and access to comfort items such as blankets. A budget airline, on the other hand, unbundles these services by offering the core service of transporting passengers from one destination to another and charging for all other additions. This helps decrease the cost of accessing the core service or component, as customers may feel that they are over-charged and over-served with services and components that they do not need.

Unbundling appeals to customers who like to cherry-pick, or those who would like to pay the minimum for core services and components. The model can therefore be considered as an a-la-carte model where the customer only pays for what he or she picks. The consumer has control over what he buys and pays for, and this is what makes unbundling work.

The decision to unbundle depends on a variety of factors. The type of industry you operate in as well as the nature of products and services offered is an important determinant. Products that are easily digitizable such as music are good candidates for unbundling: Albums can be unbundled to individual songs. Some products that manifest in physical form cannot be unbundled as easily and effectively. For instance, a physical textbook is not a good candidate for unbundling unlike its digital equivalent which can be sold in chapters.

Other considerations, such as other products in the bundle, previous sales history, whether the components in the bundle have uneven usage, and whether there will be additional value for the customer if the component is offered as a standalone,[18] should be evaluated before you decide on this model. Nevertheless, unbundling presents an opportunity for you to reprice your products to appeal to customers who may be more price-sensitive or want access to only a sub-set of the services you offer.

Freemium model

A model widely used by content providers is called "freemium", which combines the words "free" and "premium". Freemium gained popularity as a novel revenue model with the proliferation of digital and web-based offerings. The basic idea is to provide standard offerings for free. This helps to build a large user base quickly and enable the firm to earn advertisement revenues. They can also gain access to user information which in turn can be leveraged for other purposes. The business can offer a fee-based access to premium content or features (Anderson, 2008).

Successful premium models include Zoom, the multi device audio and video call and meeting provider. Founded in 2011, Zoom is an online collaboration tool that helps consolidate communications, connect people, and foster collaboration in a variety of settings.[19] With the mission of making communications frictionless and secure, Zoom adopts a freemium model. They offer basic services including virtual meetings for up to 100 people for 40 minutes, whiteboard and team chat facilities, and file sharing for free. The paid version supports larger groups, longer meetings, and cloud storage.[20]

---

[18] https://www.linkedin.com/pulse/cycle-bundling-unbundling-business-strategy-olumide-durotoluwa

[19] https://explore.zoom.us/en/about/

[20] https://zoom.us/pricing

The razor and blade model

King Camp Gillette and his amazing razor were the first disruptors of the grooming industry.[21] In 1903, when he first invented the disposable blade, King Gillette sold just 51 razors and 168 blades. Disappointed with the sales, Gillette decided to sell razors for a throw away price to the army. He also gave them away for free with Wrigley's chewing gum, coffee, tea, spices, and marshmallows. The profits came from the sale of blades that followed (Matzler, Veider, and Katham, 2015).

The Gillette model where the razor is offered at a low price whereas the consumable that goes with it — the blades — is set at a higher price; soon caught the attention of the business world. The model ensures a steady and recurrent stream of revenue for the company and came to be called the razor and blade model.

Many businesses such as manufacturers of inkjet printers, coffee machines, and PlayStation have been using the strategy successfully (Matzler *et al.*, 2013). Selling razors at a low cost ensnares the customer who has no use for it unless he purchases the more highly priced blades on a regular basis. This strategy also ensures that you decrease the barriers to entry for your customers, so that you can gain a larger user base, and then offer additional products that your customers will regularly need separately.

Change your Operations

Another strategy you can consider is to make changes to your operations. One example is the dropshipping business model adopted by firms. Many traders use this method to sell online without actually owning what they are selling.

Dropshipping is a retail fulfillment method where the seller (or dropshipper) accepts orders from customers but does not stock or own any inventory. The dropshipper receives an order and informs supplier of the order; supplier fulfills the order. These suppliers

---

[21] https://gillette.com/en-us/about/our-story

could be the authorized dealers who receive goods directly from the manufacturers or even the manufacturers themselves.[22]

In this model the "dropshipper" takes care of marketing and answering the customer's queries. They do not handle the product directly nor do they have control over stock and order fulfillment. A dropshipper's profit is determined by the difference between the retail price paid by the customer and the wholesale price charged by the supplier.

This benefits the suppliers because orders can come in from all over the world through the dropshippers; however, the risks include currency fluctuations and increasing freight charges. The dropshipper benefits from low-cost operations, as they do not stock inventory. Customers benefit because they are able to buy products at lower prices. On the downside, the business model can be easily copied and there are low barriers to entry.

Dropshipping service sources for the cheapest products from different authorized sellers all over the world based on favorable exchange rates or purchase terms. The dropshipper can determine his own price structures based on quantity sold and charge the suppliers fulfilment fees for each order.[23]

> *Are there ways to make incremental changes to your current business model, such as changing the revenue model, or making changes to the operations?*

5. Pandemic Business Models

The pandemic brought about significant impact that necessitated major amendments to business models. Businesses were shaped by restrictions imposed on movement and physical proximity, group numbers. There were additional health and hygiene precautions put in place which added to the burden on businesses. Additionally,

---

[22] https://sell.amazon.com.sg/blog/dropshipping-singapore
[23] https://www.straitstimes.com/business/invest/dropshipping-what-online-shoppers-and-sellers-should-know

there were changes in consumer preferences, lifestyle, and habits which were in turn shaped by the restrictions.

Consumers came to expect more tech-convergent shopping experiences where integrated single interfaces unify all the processes throughout their journey. Therefore, higher customer expectations in terms of personalization and interactive engagement ensue. Crowd-based models that leverage the power of the collective also emerged stronger. These models incorporate the potential of crowd thinking, crowd capability, and crowd behaviors to create new markets and workarounds in the face of constraints ecountered.

Social awareness and environmental responsibility will likely feature strongly in future business models. As the global population prepares for a future pandemic, there is a heightened awareness of climate change and sustainability which will drive businesses.[24]

One of the new concepts that has also emerged post-pandemic is the transition toward a Low-Touch Economy. It is defined as the new state of the society and economy, which has been changed by the COVID-19 pandemic and characterized "by low-touch interactions, health and safety measures, new human behaviors, and permanent industry shifts".[25] The restrictions placed on physical interaction presented opportunities for companies to search for solutions to circumvent these. Technology played an important role in this area, enabling transition of brick-and-mortar stores to go online and continue to serve their customers. Thermal screening technology, sensor-based solutions, digital wallets, and voice activated agents helped to enhance safety of physical stores.

Simultaneously on the part of the consumers, the establishment of the "new normal" post-pandemic has brought about transforma-

---

[24] https://www.globenewswire.com/en/news-release/2022/01/13/2366185/28124/en/Business-Model-Innovation-Post-COVID-19-2021-Report-Outcome-as-a-service-Model-Drives-Value-Chain-Compression-and-Transforms-Customer-to-a-Partner-for-OEMs.html

[25] https://www.boardofinnovation.com/blog/what-is-the-low-touch-economy/

tion in their purchasing patterns and habits. Post-pandemic, customers are more willing to try new products and new ways of transacting. We will discuss how businesses managed the pandemic in detail in our concluding chapter.

As we transition to a post-pandemic economy, what are some of the changes that can be made to your business model?

Chapter 10

Surviving the Pandemic

"When written in Chinese, the word crisis is composed of two characters —
one represents danger, and the other represents opportunity."
— *John F. Kennedy*

Throughout this book we have been looking at how the pandemic has forced changes to various aspects of running a business. In this chapter, we present specific findings from our research on some of the coping strategies adopted by small businesses to combat the pandemic. We also present the key lessons distilled from the cases we examined which would prepare businesses for future shocks they may face.

COVID-19 was one of the worst pandemic events in human history with the World Health Organization reporting, 584,065,952 confirmed cases including 6,418,958 deaths as of 10 August 2022.[1] Now, as the disease has come to be accepted as endemic in parts of the world, governments, businesses, and societies at large need to reconcile with the fact that some of its effects may be here to stay. So, what are some of the strategies used by businesses to manage the restrictions imposed to control the pandemic? How are small and medium enterprises coping compared to their larger counterparts?

---

[1] https://covid19.who.int/

These questions need to be looked at carefully, given the risk of another pandemic strike or another external shock is very real.

1. Impact of COVID-19

One of the initial actions undertaken by governments to combat the pandemic included travel restrictions and lockdowns. Social distancing between people out in public spaces was also enforced as a precaution against the communal spread of infection; workplaces moved to an arrangement where employees were required to work from home (WFH). Changes were mandated to all customer-facing activities of business entities and organizations due to the additional sanitation and safety requirements imposed.

According to a World Bank report, the impact of these measures worldwide was threefold: The first was a drop in employment due to lower availability of labor. Factory closures and workers staying home resulted in idle resources and underutilization of capacity in factories. The second impact was the rise in costs of imports and exports across many goods and services. The third shock was a sharp drop in international tourism. Travel agents were affected as travel bookings were cut in half by March 2020. Airlines worldwide lost billions in revenue as global travel plummeted. There was a drop in household consumption as consumers purchased fewer services requiring close human interaction, such as mass transport, domestic tourism, restaurant dine-in, and recreational activities. Demand was redirected towards consumption of other goods and services including online shopping and entertainment (Maliszewska, Mattoo, and van der Mensbrugghe, 2022).

Products and services were naturally prioritized as essentials and non-essentials with the result that those that fell in the latter category had to face more serious consequences of the drop in demand. Essential goods and services such as food, medical products, and services as well as health and sanitation services saw an unprecedented surge in demand, which posed its own unique challenges.

Globally, consumer packaged goods companies faced more pressure than ever. This was partly due to the increase in prices of food and packaging commodities as well as a rise in manufacturing wages and labor costs.[2] In Singapore, the pandemic led to decline in travel service exports, which included goods and services consumed by travelers to Singapore. However, there were positive contributions from the exports of other business services, telecommunications, computer and information services, and financial services.[3]

Organizations and businesses went into an overdrive mode for survival. However, this was easier said than done. Companies needed to transform by making radical changes to their operating models to remain agile. They also needed to reinvent themselves though digital transformation, tweaking products and services, target markets, and supply chain partners, and by establishing variable cost structures.

2. The Pandemic Archetypes

Our research on the impact of COVID-19 amongst small and medium enterprises helped to develop a classification of three typical archetypes based on the nature of the business, impact of covid, and the coping mechanisms adopted as follows (Ravindran and Boh, 2020):

The Pandemic Warrior archetype consists of companies dealing in products and services classified as essentials during a pandemic situation. As such, these firms depend heavily on people and are required to remain operational in person even during a pandemic. With demand surges for their products and services, it may seem like they are in a position to exploit this surge. But in reality, they have to face their own unique challenges: Surging demand, staffing issues, and supply chain disruptions. Pandemic warriors are on the

---

[2] https://www.mckinsey.com/business-functions/risk-and-resilience/our-insights/covid-19-implications-for-business

[3] https://www.mti.gov.sg/Resources/feature-articles/2022/Impact-of-the-COVID-19-Pandemic-on-Singapore-Services-Export#:~:text=As%20a%20result%2C%20the%20value,6.7%20per%20cent%20in%202021.

frontlines and are seen combating pandemic challenges on a daily basis.

The Survivor archetype is so called because they are constantly striving to stay relevant during a time when priorities change. This is because they deal in products and services that are non-essential and they are acutely affected by the sudden drop in demand. This group may depend heavily on manpower resources and physical spaces and strategies to keep their business relevant and visible during the crisis. Yet, many of them are resilient and pivot to new products and services that are in greater demand. They also switch to alternate channels to reach their target audience. Survivors remain flexible and adapt to the changing conditions, which gives them a much higher chance of surviving in a crisis.

The Digital Native is the type of firm that exploits opportunities digitally due to the fundamental nature and distinct capabilities of their business. Firms recognized the importance of digital technologies and solutions in the face of the movement restrictions imposed during the pandemic. This places a group of companies that already deal in digital services at a special advantage. The digital native is characterized by their nimbleness as well as the speed with which they are able to adapt to changing situations. The structure and existing mode of working allows them this flexibility. The firms thus can continue operating and are able to exploit the general trend of digitalization to their benefit. Nevertheless, they may have their own unique challenges to combat in doing so. For instance, changes in the marketplace may add pressure on this group and they may be forced to put profits behind community outreach and ensuring customer welfare.

3. Coping Strategies

So, what are some of the coping strategies adopted by firms that have had to manage the challenges posed by the spread of COVID-19? Multiple strategies have been adopted by firms to cope with the pandemic as illustrated in Figure 1. Firms have resorted to changes to their products and services and target market in a bid to combat the

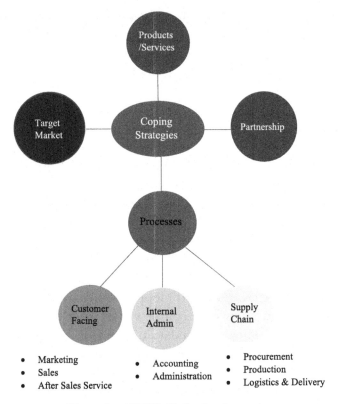

Figure 1: COVID-19 Coping Strategies

pandemic. They have also tweaked key processes such as marketing, sales, and service besides transforming support processes that enable production and delivery. Supply chain processes, stores and distribution facilities as well as partnerships have undergone drastic changes.

Modify/Tweak Products/Services

The pandemic has forced firms to diversify and come up with alternative products or service lines. One of the strategies reported by firms is repurposing current products, services, and resources. For example, a coffee making company we spoke with decided to allow customers to use their idle coffee equipment for free with purchase of their coffee. This was because the machinery was underutilized as orders reduced dramatically during the pandemic. This strategy allowed the firm to add value to their offerings. At the same time, the resulting additional costs were negligible as the firm was utilizing available resources that were left idle during the lull period.

Leveraging competencies

The pandemic forced restrictions on businesses that often rendered their core competencies useless. For instance, large events were banned almost all over the world and businesses that focused on such events, suffered huge losses. One of the strategies adopted by such event management firms was to leverage their expertise in domains of greater demand — digital media production, while defocusing on other expertise. For example, one event management firm we examined dropped their stalled projects and moved on to focus on providing digital media production services. They switched to digital content creation and stepped out and onto the social media space where their core competencies were still relevant and could be applied. They switched to organizing live webinars, producing educational videos, or creating marketing videos for firms who were challenged to start advertising digitally.

In exploiting capabilities, firms could also provide new services. For instance, as more and more firms adopted digitalization, customers who previously may not have had any experience with online interactions may have had to adapt to using online services. Some firms adapted to the COVID-19 situation by offering technical support or instructional material to help customers use newly implemented services online.

Provide in-demand products

One of the strategies adopted by pandemic hit firms was to pivot into entirely new products and services that may see a sudden surge in demand during the time. This is because, even as many products and services were made redundant, demand for new products and services sprang up during the pandemic. We came across several examples that illustrated this strategy.

For example, a company specializing in cleaning solutions used their know-how to make disinfectants for COVID-19. An accounting software company started offering new services to help clients modernize their accounting processes and automate their workflow in a bid to remain in business.

One of the interviewees, Jimmy D'Souza, and his wife, Emily D'Souza, own and run FairDeal Private Ltd, a dealership of Honeywell home security systems from Bangalore, India. The firm employed three staff members who helped them with sales, installation, after sales service, and operations. The systems were sold to housing estates and office complexes in and around the city and the company had enjoyed a fairly smooth ride since its establishment in 2011.

However, COVID-19 was extremely challenging for the company. The firm experienced a sudden drop in customer demand as the situation worsened. Apartment complexes, schools, institutions, and office complexes which constituted their regular client base had new priorities such as ensuring the safety of their users and tenants. One of the strategies Jimmy used to get the business back on track was to diversify the product offerings of FairDeal. Jimmy noticed that Honeywell had a range of products, some of which were of interest due to the special characteristics of the situation. He saw the trend towards increasing demand for systems that enabled contactless authentication using technologies such as face recognition as well as for thermometers and temperature scanners. Jimmy decided to quickly move in to capitalize on this opportunity. He stocked up on these items in a bid to make good the shortfall in sales of the home security systems. In addition, Jimmy also shifted his focus to the company's training wing, which dealt with value engineering — a pandemic safe option. As noted by Jimmy, "after all training could still be offered through various online interactive platforms freely available such as Zoom."

Redefining the Target Market

Firms also resorted to a strategy of targeting new customer segments in a bid to overcome the restrictions posed by COVID-19 and to remain viable. This is especially true of businesses that suffered due to movement restrictions as well as lockdowns enforced by local governments.

An example can be seen in the case of LZ, a Malaysian firm in the business of providing digital signages. Digital signage uses technologies such as LCD and LED display and projection to display images and videos using a content management system. These are usually found in public spaces and corporate offices and widely used by businesses, organizations, and government bodies. Some common locations include exhibitions and conferences, transportation systems, museums, airports, stadiums, highways, malls, and stores.

Smart digital signage solutions integrate third party content with customized content aimed to attract potential customers and audience. LZ was initially targeting hotels and malls by providing indoor digital signage to companies. The problem, however, was that their clients were severely affected by the pandemic and the local government ordering a movement control order (MCO).

The company pivoted early when the pandemic hit and, in five months, implemented the change. They switched to outdoor signages and shifted their focus to a new target audience — SMEs owning shop lots, which are abundant in Malaysia — instead of continuing to look for traditional malls and hotels.

In some instances, the business may come to a standstill due to restrictions as demand dips to zero. We found cases of firms that shifted focus from their regular clientele to the community at large during the peak of the pandemic to do their bit for the society and remain visible. Beijing-based Oriental Nexus is a web platform for entrepreneurs and investors to come together and identify mutually beneficial business opportunities. The firm has around 3,500 venture capitalists and 100 million businesses on their platform, including big names such as Alibaba. Additionally, Oriental caters to provincial government initiatives, organizing events and roadshows aimed at attracting business investments in the territories. Such events constitute a major proportion of their business.

The biggest challenge that the company faced with the COVID-19 outbreak was the sudden stoppage of all government organized events and roadshows, one of the company's mainstays.

This was further aggravated by the fact that payments for the completed government projects were also suspended since the provincial governments had other priorities. Faced with these challenges, the company focused its attention on what could be done that would be of use to the community given the gravity of the situation.

According to Daniel Ong, the founder,

> *"One of the things we did during this period was to look at creating brand awareness. We worked on developing a site on how businesses could tackle the COVID situation. We also consolidated information about stimulus packages and governmental schemes — a one-stop information center of sorts." (Ravindran and Boh, 2020).*

Modifying Business Processes

Enhancing or improving business process is a major strategy adopted to manage the challenges of pandemic restrictions as we discussed in the chapter on digital transformation. Since face-to-face meetings got difficult due to safety concerns, most customer-facing processes such as marketing, sales, and service were transformed. Virtual processes using mobile and Internet technologies as well as other telecommunication facilities replaced conventional physical processes. This was the case even with established brick-and-mortar businesses that previously had very little motivation to adopt online processes. Small businesses such as mini marts and small shops in Singapore scrambled to adopt virtual product catalogues and mobile payment options. Many firms saw an opportunity to legitimize and push for more streamlined and efficient processes using digital technologies during the pandemic.

Take the case of Veda Organics set up by Amit Singh to promote a pioneer brand selling organically grown Indian spices, lentils, grains, and cereals within the United States of America. The business dealt with essential goods and the problems faced during the pandemic primarily included having to manage a surge in demand with a supply chain that was interrupted by various bottlenecks and disruptions. Amit saw that there was a need to diversify their distribution channels and ensure that a portion of his goods would be sold through ecommerce. He noted:

> *"I never really paid much attention to e-commerce. We only had a small presence on Amazon until now as the prices were high and my customers would much rather pick up the items in store. However, this pandemic situation has urged me to push Amazon sales, so I ensured more stock is allocated on this channel. I now realize that this is an aspect I have to consciously push, in order to be better prepared for a pandemic."(Ravindran and Boh, 2020).*

As for supply chains, they have been redefined since the pandemic spread globally. Two of the major events that forced the business world to rethink their supply chains was the supply shock that originated in China when the pandemic first showed up and the demand shock that originated in the rest of the world due to lockdowns and restrictions as the disease spread. One significant trend is the general inward focus and weaning off of global supply chains. This forced manufacturers who were under political pressures to increase their domestic production to ensure jobs went to people in their home countries. Organizations also scurried to reduce or even eliminate their dependence on sources that are perceived as risky. This meant that inventory held in global supply chains was reduced in a reversal of trend.[4]

In general, companies made strategic changes to the structure, configuration, and operation of their supply chains. There may be differences in the exact strategies used from sector to sector. For example, McKinsey reports that healthcare players regionalized their supply chains by moving production closer to end markets. The automotive, aerospace, and defense players were slower to adopt these supply chain changes, but many still implemented them to ensure survival.

The pandemic pushed risk to the top of virtually every corporate agenda. Formal supply chain risk management processes were given emphasis post pandemic. Some built up supply chain risk

---

[4] https://hbr.org/2020/09/global-supply-chains-in-a-post-pandemic-world

management practices from scratch, while others adopted new ones or strengthened their existing capabilities.[5]

For smaller firms, a shortage of staff either due to staff cuts or the fact that they could not work on site forced them to implement processes such as virtual training where necessary. Tasks such as maintenance and even medical consultation went virtual, supported by AI and other automation tools.

Changes in Partnerships

Just as supply chains underwent a strategic shift, partnerships also had to undergo changes. Old partnerships that did not work well in the changed situation had to be discontinued and new ones were forged to garner the support needed to work around restrictions. Many firms found themselves in need of technical or domain expertise and sought the help of vendors to manage the new business process requirements. Thus, new partnerships were formed with specialists in the digital space to enable digital transformation, digital and social media marketing, and event organization.

We spoke to firms who were dependent on influencers for the promotion of their fashion accessories. However, due to COVID-19 restrictions, these influencers were unable to shoot promotional videos outdoors. The company soon made a shift to engage their customers as their marketers with the help of pictures and testimonials.

In another example, a firm that originally was into training pivoted to selling visitor management system as there was a demand for such systems during the pandemic. This meant that they had to forge new partnerships with specialists in facial recognition and thermal scanning to implement the system.

How do you Ensure Pandemic Readiness?

According to a World Bank report, firms that survived the COVID-19 crisis were older and more productive; they also tended to be

---

[5] https://www.mckinsey.com/business-functions/operations/our-insights/how-covid-19-is-reshaping-supply-chains

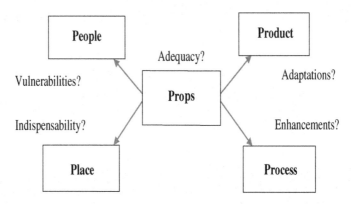

Figure 2:   Pandemic Readiness Audit

Source: Ravindran and Boh, 2020.

innovators and operated in less challenging business environments. In what can be termed a "Schumpeterian cleansing," less productive firms permanently shut down operations during the crisis. Those who remained standing were characterized by higher productivity levels.[6] Yet, even as the world settles down to a new economic order, the effect of the pandemic lingers on and serves as a reminder to firms to be prepared for any such future events.

So, what can you do to make sure that you are not caught unawares if a pandemic or another external shock strikes again in the future? We derived an audit check list that can be used to assess pandemic readiness of firms from our analysis of the interviews done with businesses that are covid survivors (Ravindran and Boh, 2020). An overview of how these checks can be done is illustrated in Figure 2.

Think People — People, whether it is employees, customers, or supply chain partners, need to be taken care of as the first priority. People issues feature in almost all cases, in the form of employee fears and insecurities. Staff often reported anxieties about catching the infection as the firms remained operational during the pandemic.

Lockdown measures have an immediate impact on the daily routines of employees, forcing them to put in place alternate work

---

[6] https://blogs.worldbank.org/developmenttalk/surviving-pandemic-business-perspective

arrangements. Supply chain partners also had to be managed in order to ensure supplies could meet the surge in demand. The "Digital Natives" had less difficulty in keeping in touch with customers as they had the means to reach out and are also naturally fast adapters.

Businesses need to identify how each of their stakeholders will be affected by the pandemic and assess whether they have the means to allay their concerns and be able to engage with them effectively during the period.

Think Products — Products make the key difference between survival and closure during a pandemic, as is illustrated by the archetypes presented. What type of products and services does the firm deal in? Is this considered essential or non-essential in a pandemic situation is an important question to ask.

Studying government guidelines regarding what constitutes essentials during a pandemic situation could be a good starting point. Thus, for businesses that identify themselves as clearly non-essential in a pandemic situation, it is important to see if there would be elements of the existing products or services that could still be relevant to the changing market needs and within the new restrictions that come into effect.

Think Processes — How flexible are your key business processes in supporting the changes required to customize or change the products and services offered during a pandemic? This question needs to be asked.

Even if you are dealing in essential products for which demand surges during a pandemic, it is important to get a backup supply chain ready and running. This is because it will be impossible to capitalize on the additional demand unless you have ready and uninterrupted supplies. Therefore, supply chains need to be tested for responsiveness and stockpiles have to be reassessed in preparation for a pandemic situation. Logistics chains also need to be assessed to ensure uninterrupted delivery.

Firms on the frontlines also identify the difficulties in incorporating additional sanitization and hygiene practices into their day-to-day operations. Therefore, they need to take stock of customer/outward facing processes that support the main operations. They also need to identify and evaluate their readiness in terms of resources for all the additional processes that may be needed during a pandemic: Temperature scanning, sanitization of work desks, and contact tracing.

Think Places — The COVID-19 crisis has shifted focus from physical spaces to virtual ones, whether it is home offices for employees (WFH), or virtual platforms to interact with clients. It is important for firms to evaluate their readiness and capabilities in using such virtual spaces. Virtual spaces will play a more dominant role in the post-COVID-19 new normal, and firms will need to reassess the relative proportion of physical and virtual spaces they plan to use in order to be prepared.

Think Props — A firm relies on a variety of things for its efficient and effective functioning. This supporting infrastructure includes information systems, telecommunication components as well as transport and delivery vehicles and can be called props. During a pandemic as the firm tweaks its products and processes, props should be able to adapt accordingly. Hence, it is important to ask if you have the props for employees to work remotely, contact customers, and deliver their modified products and services effectively.

Summary

Through the ten chapters of the book, we took you through the entrepreneurial journey starting with the search for business ideas and opportunities through to execution of the idea, developing novel business models to shape and structure the business, adopting appropriate business strategies, and leveraging on emerging trends to remain viable and relevant. Insights into selection and management of partnerships as a key process in establishing a strong enterprise as well as pointers on how a business may manage the challenges posed by a pandemic situation are also discussed.

As far as ideation is concerned, there are many sources from which you can gain inspiration. The key take away would be to look inward at your own problems, look outward at the pain points of your major stakeholders, or look beyond into unfamiliar territories for novel ideas. Problems are right at the center of your search for viable business ideas. Additionally, available solutions that are currently ineffective, hacks and workarounds as well as major socio-economic and technological trends that have the potential to bring about a paradigm shift could inspire you to come up with ideas that may be developed into a viable new business.

A design thinking approach can be used to translate your business idea into a working project or a full-fledged venture. The points to remember are to understand and clearly define the problem you are addressing, applying principles such as human centricity and tolerance for ambiguity while at the same time adopting a structured and action-oriented approach embracing a collaborative spirit. The key is to focus on the user and his or her context with empathy and understand the problem rather than jump to a solution prematurely. It is also important to put aside what the user says he or she wants or what the business perceives to be their need. Encouraging creative and diverse ideas will ensure that you will be successful in your mission to find the best solution that addresses the defined problem.

We also remind you that besides looking to discover business opportunities, you could actively create opportunities for yourselves. These two approaches to opportunity identification — through (1) discovery and (2) creation — are complementary in nature. You can create business opportunities through resource combination and bricolage which in summary is about "making do". In this approach, you apply innovative combinations of resources you already have to create new opportunities that did not exist previously. In doing so it helps to be frugal, seek help from external agencies wherever needed, and avoid reinventing the wheel. You may also need to be open to transforming your goals as you go through the exercise.

Contingency exploitation and options generation are two approaches that help firms to manage unpredictable events that may unfold in the course of their entrepreneurial journey. Contingency exploitation refers to converting a crisis to an opportunity by cultivating a capability for "strategic reactiveness". Options generation is about developing various fallback options in the face of volatility. This demands a certain level of flexibility so that you can readily switch from Plan A to Plan B when the situation warrants. Needless to say, businesses need to remain agile and amenable to changes in the face of contingencies.

Partnerships are vital as the entrepreneurship journey can be difficult without the support of external stakeholders. Partnerships also help firms acquire the necessary social capital and to achieve synergies. Social capital is made of (1) Structural capital that reflects the advantages derived from the structure of your network; (2) Relational capital which refers to the resources that are accessible to you based on the depth of connections; and (3) Cognitive capital refers to the extent to which you share common goals and a common understanding with your connections so that they can support you meaningfully. There are several factors to consider in partnership selection and management. Selection of partners often depends on your personal preferences, values, and business needs. You can also choose and select partners based on task-related or partner-related criteria. The former focuses on operational skills: Aspects that are important to your organization's competitive success. The latter, pertains to the partner's ability to cooperate effectively with your organization. A partnership model defines approaches towards forming and managing the partnership over time. It also suggests what approach you should take towards building cooperation and trust as well as establishing communication. You can adopt a range of models starting with informal to flexible and symbiotic to manage your partnerships.

The pandemic has been pushing through a digitally driven transformation that has resulted in the emergence of an entirely new world order. Digital Transformation emerged as a recent trend embraced by many businesses in a bid to exploit emerging technologies such as AI and IoT for growth and adaptation. Tools such as chatbots and applications such as IoT have revolutionized the way a business can engage with their target audience. The specific affordances and characteristics of this suite of technologies and applications including immersiveness and personalization, intelligent sensing, ubiquity and accessibility, and reconfigurability provide interesting new ways of serving your target audience as illustrated by the numerous successful business cases. Each of these characteristics singularly or collectively presents opportunities for you to overhaul your fundamental model or to make radical changes to the way your enterprise operates.

Emerging trends inspire business opportunities in that they provide a general direction for you to move ahead. Changes such as increasing longevity and youth demographics set new needs and expectations for businesses to meet. The younger customers prefer to rent than to own and are impatient when it comes to services. They prefer to be served anywhere, anytime, and low wait times is a basic expectation. Platform mediated trust has accelerated a trend towards sharing models and the emergence of a gig economy and these in turn have introduced new ways of value propositioning for entrepreneurs.

Consequently, several disruptive and innovative business models have emerged in the recent years, redefining entire industry sectors and you can learn from them. Business models are the basic blueprints of an executable business idea, and it is important for businesses to spell this out upfront to define and understand the interactions between what they offer, to whom, and how so that they can remain economically viable. Some of the novel and successful business models could potentially inspire entirely new ideas or provide useful tips on how you could tweak and realign your own models. Various sharing models, product as a service model, and the classic razor and blade model and the spin on it are some examples.

Finally, there are valuable lessons to be learnt from the pandemic experience which will help you to prepare for yet another crisis in future. As a first step, your business could identify the category of enterprise it belongs to on the basis of your pandemic experience. You can then go on to identify the specific challenges you will face should another crisis strike. As they say, "fore-warned is fore-armed" and this will give you a heads up when it comes to combating another external shock such as COVID-19. A check list of items that will ensure preparedness of an enterprise in dealing with a pandemic situation is also included which will ensure you are combat ready.

Overall, we hope that the principles and examples provided in this book will help you identify and develop new business opportunities and ensure your enterprise is managed successfully through the turmoil of an unpredictable economic environment that you traverse.

References

Chapter 1

Kononets, Y. and Treiblmaier, H. (2021). The Potential of Bio Certification to Strengthen the Market Position of Food Producers. *Modern Supply Chain Research and Applications*, *3*(1), p. 41–55.

Sarasvathy, S.D., Dew, N., Velamuri, S.R., & Venkataraman, S. (2003). Three Views of Entrepreneurial Opportunity. In *Handbook of Entrepreneurship Research*. Springer, p. 141–160.

Chapter 2

von Hippel, E. (2016). *Free Innovation*. The MIT Press, Cambridge, MA.

Chapter 3

Auh, S. and Menguc, B. (2005). Top Management Team Diversity and Innovativeness: The Moderating Role of Interfunctional Coordination. *Industrial Marketing Management*, *34*(3), p. 249–261.

Kolko, J. (2015). *Design Thinking Comes of Age*. Harvard Business Publishing Education.

Liedtka, J., King, A., and Bennett, K. (2013). *Solving Problems With Design Thinking: Ten Stories of What Works*. Columbia University Press.

Razzouk, R. and Shute, V. (2012). What is Design Thinking and Why is it Important? *Review of Educational Research, 82*(3), p. 330–348.

Schumpeter, J.A. (1982). *The Theory of Economic Development: An Inquiry Into Profits, Capital, Credit, Interest, and the Business Cycle (1912/1934)*. Transaction Publishers, London, p. 244.

Sethi, R., Smith, D.C., and Park, C.W. (2001). Cross-Functional Product Development Teams, Creativity, and the Innovativeness of New Consumer Products. *Journal of Marketing Research, 38*(1), p. 73–85.

Simon, H.A. (1969). *The Sciences of the Artificial.* The MIT Press, Cambridge MA.

Talke, K., Salomo, S., and Rost, K. (2010). How Top Management Team Diversity Affects Innovativeness and Performance via the Strategic Choice to Focus on Innovation Fields. *Research Policy, 39*(7), p. 907–918.

Chapter 4

Alvarez, S.A. and Barney, J.B. (2007). Discovery and Creation: Alternative Theories of Entrepreneurial Action. *Strategic Entrepreneurship Journal, 1*(1–2), p. 11–26.

Baker, T. and Nelson, R.E. (2005). Creating Something from Nothing: Resource Construction Through Entrepreneurial Bricolage. *Administrative Science Quarterly, 50*(3), p. 329–366.

Barney, J., Wright, M., and Ketchen Jr, D.J. (2001). The Resource-Based View of the Firm: Ten Years After 1991. *Journal of Management, 27*(6), p. 625.

Kirzner, I.M. (1973). *Competition and Entrepreneurship.* University of Chicago Press, Chicago.

Lévi-Strauss, C. (1968). *The Savage Mind.* University of Chicago Press, Chicago.

Sarasvathy, S.D. (2001). Causation and Effectuation: Toward a Theoretical Shift from Economic Inevitability to Entrepreneurial Contingency. *Academy of Management Review, 26*(2), p. 243–263.

Senyard, J., Baker, T., Steffens, P., and Davidsson, P. (2014). Bricolage as a Path to Innovativeness for Resource-Constrained New Firms. *Journal of Product Innovation Management, 31*(2), p. 211–230.

Chapter 5

Sarasvathy, S.D. (2001). Causation and Effectuation: Toward a Theoretical Shift from Economic Inevitability to Entrepreneurial Contingency. *Academy of management Review*, *26*(2), p. 243–263.

Taleb, N.N. (2007). Black Swans and the Domains of Statistics. *The American Statistician*, *61*(3), p. 198–200.

Chapter 6

Dentoni, D., Pinkse, J., and Lubberink, R. (2021). Linking Sustainable Business Models to Socio-Ecological Resilience Through Cross-Sector Partnerships: A Complex Adaptive Systems View. *Business & Society*, *60*(5), p. 1216–1252.

Geringer, J.M. (1991). Strategic Determinants of Partner Selection Criteria in International Joint Ventures. *Journal of International Business Studies*, *22*(1), p. 41–62.

Ghadimi, P., Toosi, F.G., and Heavey, C. (2018). A Multi-Agent Systems Approach for Sustainable Supplier Selection and Order Allocation in a Partnership Supply Chain. *European Journal of Operational Research*, *269*(1), p. 286–301.

Lasker, R.D., Weiss, E.S., and Miller, R. (2001). Partnership Synergy: A Practical Framework for Studying and Strengthening the Collaborative Advantage. *The Milbank Quarterly*, *79*(2), p. 179–205.

Moen, Ø., Bolstad, A., Pedersen, V., and Bakås, O. (2010). International Market Expansion Strategies for High-Tech Firms: Partnership Selection Criteria for Forming Strategic Alliances. *International Journal of Business and Management*, *5*(1), p. 20.

Tuten, T.L. and Urban, D.J. (2001). An Expanded Model of Business-to-Business Partnership Formation and Success. *Industrial Marketing Management*, *30*(2), p. 149–164.

Yunus, M., Moingeon, B., and Lehmann-Ortega, L. (2010). Building Social Business Models: Lessons from the Grameen Experience. *Long Range Planning*, *43*(2–3), p. 308–325.

Zhu, S.X. (2015). Analysis of Dual Sourcing Strategies Under Supply Disruptions. *International Journal of Production Economics*, *170*, p. 191–203.

Chapter 7

Arthur, W.B. (2009). *The Nature of Technology: What it is and How it Evolves.* Simon and Schuster.

Guha, A., Grewal, D., Kopalle, P.K., Haenlein, M., Schneider, M.J., Jung, H., ... Hawkins, G. (2021). How Artificial Intelligence Will Affect the Future of Retailing. *Journal of Retailing, 97*(1), p. 28–41.

Liu, J. (2021). Social Robots as the Bride?: Understanding the Construction of Gender in a Japanese Social Robot Product. *Human-Machine Communication, 2*, p. 105–120.

Morakanyane, R., Grace, A.A., and O'reilly, P. (2017). Conceptualizing Digital Transformation in Business Organizations: A Systematic Review of Literature. *Bled eConference, 21*, p. 428–444.

Nambisan, S. (2017). Digital Entrepreneurship: Toward a Digital Technology Perspective of Entrepreneurship. *Entrepreneurship Theory and Practice, 41*(6), p. 1029–1055.

Pandit, N., Prox, C., and Baldwin, C.Y. (2022). Studying Modular Design: An Interview With Carliss Y. Baldwin. *Journal of Organization Design, 11*(2), p. 77–85.

White, D. and Galbraith, P.W. (2019). Japan's Emerging Emotional Tech. *Anthropology News, 60*(1), p. e41–e47.

Zidi, S., Hamani, N., Samir, B., and Kermad, L. (2022). Use of Fuzzy Logic for Reconfigurability Assessment in Supply Chain. *International Journal of Fuzzy Systems, 24*(2), p. 1025–1045.

Chapter 8

Asioli, D., Aschemann-Witzel, J., Caputo, V., Vecchio, R., Annunziata, A., Næs, T., and Varela, P. (2017). Making Sense of the "Clean Label" Trends: A Review of Consumer Food Choice Behavior and Discussion of Industry Implications. *Food Research International, 99*, p. 58–71.

Bocken, N.M.P., de Pauw, I., Bakker, C., and van der Grinten, B. (2016). Product Design and Business Model Strategies for a Circular Economy. *Journal of Industrial and Production Engineering, 33* (5), p. 308–320.

Boh, W.F., Ren, Y., Kiesler, S., and Bussjaeger, R. (2007). Expertise and Collaboration in the Geographically Dispersed Organization. *Organization Science, 18*(4), p. 595–612.

Choudary, S.P., Parker, G.G., and van Alstyne, M. (2015). *Platform Scale: How an Emerging Business Model Helps Startups Build Large Empires With Minimum Investment.* Platform Thinking Labs.

de Chiara, A. (2016). Eco-Labeled Products: Trend or Tools for Sustainability Strategies? *Journal of Business Ethics*, *137*(1), p. 161–172.

Dingli, A. and Seychell, D. (2015). *Who are the digital natives?*. In *The New Digital Natives*. Springer, p. 9–22.

Homrich, A.S., Galvão, G., Abadia, L.G., and Carvalho, M.M. (2018). The Circular Economy Umbrella: Trends and Gaps on Integrating Pathways. *Journal of Cleaner Production*, *175*, p. 525–543.

Kaine, S. and Josserand, E. (2019). The Organisation and Experience of Work in the Gig Economy. *Journal of Industrial Relations*, *61*(4), p. 479–501.

Manyika, J., Lund, S., Bughin, J., Robinson, K., Mischke, J., and Mahajan, D. (2016). Independent-Work-Choice-Necessity-and-the-Gig-Economy. *McKinsey Global Institute*.

Mirabella, N., Castellani, V., and Sala, S. (2014). Current Options for the Valorization of Food Manufacturing Waste: A Review. *Journal of Cleaner Production*, *65*(Complete), p. 28–41.

Neves, M.I.L., Silva, E.K., and Meireles, M.A.A. (2021). Natural Blue Food Colorants: Consumer Acceptance, Current Alternatives, Trends, Challenges, and Future Strategies. *Trends in Food Science & Technology*, *112*, p. 163–173.

Puschmann, T. and Alt, R. (2016). Sharing Economy. *Business & Information Systems Engineering*, *58*(1), p. 93–99.

Schlagwein, D., Schoder, D., and Spindeldreher, K. (2020). Consolidated, systemic conceptualization, and definition of the "sharing economy". *Journal of the Association for Information Science and Technology*, *71*(7), p. 817–838.

Schor, J. (2016). Debating the sharing economy. *Journal of Self-Governance and Management Economics*, *4*(3), p. 7–22.

Stahel, W.R. (2016). The Circular Economy. *Nature*, *531*(7595), p. 435–438.

The Economist. (2015). *Learning to Sell Online: Cash Cow, Taobao*, in *Economist*. http://www.economist.com/news/china/21602755-one-small-hamlet-teaching-people-how-sell-online-cash-cow-taobao.

Vallandingham, L.R., Yu, Q., Sharma, N., Strandhagen, J.W., and Strandhagen, J.O. (2018). Grocery Retail Supply Chain Planning and Control: Impact of Consumer Trends and Enabling Technologies. *IFAC-PapersOnLine*, *51*(11), p. 612–617.

Vallas, S. and Schor, J.B. (2020). What Do Platforms Do? Understanding the Gig Economy. *Annual Review of Sociology*, *46*(1), p. 273–294.

Chapter 9

Anderson, C. (2008). Free! Why $0.00 is the Future of Business. *Wired Magazine, 16*(3), p. 140–149.

Brabham, D.C. (2008). Crowdsourcing as a Model for Problem Solving: An Introduction and Cases. *Convergence, 14*(1), p. 75–90.

Christensen, C.M. (2016). Know Your Customers' Jobs to be Done. *Harvard Business Review, 94*(9), p. 54–62.

Estellés-Arolas, E., Navarro-Giner, R., and González-Ladrón-de-Guevara, F. (2015). *Crowdsourcing Fundamentals: Definition and Typology*. In *Advances in Crowdsourcing*. Springer, p. 33–48.

Hanafizadeh, P. and Harati Nik, M.R. (2020). Configuration of Data Monetization: A Review of Literature With Thematic Analysis. *Global Journal of Flexible Systems Management, 21*(1), p. 17–34.

Johnson, M.W., Christensen, C.M., and Kagermann, H. (2008). Reinventing Your Business Model. *Harvard Business Review, 86*(12), p. 57–68.

Lindgardt, Z., Reeves, M., Stalk, Jr, G., and Deimler, M. (2012). *Business model innovation: When the Game Gets Tough, Change the Game*. The Boston Consulting Group, Boston, MA, p. 291–298.

Matzler, K., Bailom, F., von den Eichen, S.F., and Kohler, T. (2013). Business Model Innovation: Coffee Triumphs for Nespresso. *Journal of Business Strategy*.

Matzler, K., Veider, V., and Kathan, W. (2015). *Adapting to the Sharing Economy*. MIT Cambridge, MA.

Parvinen, P. (2020). Advancing Data Monetization and the Creation of Data-Based Business Models. *Communications of the Association for Information Systems, 47*(1), p. 2.

Chapter 10

Maliszewska, M., Mattoo, A., and van der Mensbrugghe, D. (2022). The Potential Impact of COVID-19 on GDP and Trade: A Preliminary Assessment. *Policy Research Working Paper No. 9211, World Bank, Washington, DC*.

Ravindran, T. and Boh, W.F. (2020). Lessons From COVID-19: Toward a Pandemic Readiness Audit Checklist for Small and Medium-Sized Enterprises. *IEEE Engineering Management Review, 48*(3), p. 55–62.

Index

Printed in the United States
by Baker & Taylor Publisher Services